ACCESS GRANTED

Tomorrow's Business Ethics

Vol.2

Patrick Henz

Copyright © 2017 Patrick Henz. Pictures by Patrick Henz, exceptions are marked.
Cover artwork by Patrick Henz.

All rights reserved.

ISBN: 978-1979899482
ISBN-13: 1979899487

DEDICATION

For the Reader, the Wanderer, the Scientist.

CONTENTS

	Introduction	i
1	And so it begins	10
2	Whiz Kids	14
3	More Trouble with Bubbles	19
4	Cressey 4.0	23
5	IT Diversity	27
6	Gaia	30
7	Cyberdyne	34
8	Deming's World of Tomorrow	37
9	Alien Inside	42
10	The AI Coach	47
11	Compliance New Defined	50
12	Catharsis	65
13	Machiavelli for AI	68
14	The Heart of AI	71
15	Data Privacy for the Digital Twin	73
16	Enzo 4.0 – The Digital Counselor	77
17	The Strangest Things	82
18	Artists Needed	85
19	A Day in the Future	88
20	Artificial Intelligence according to Philip K. Dick:	92

Why Androids Dream

21	Zombification	99
22	"I am a Racer"	102
23	Gamification^2	107
24	Blockchain to eliminate the Intermediate	112
25	Ethics, Compliance, Democracy & Data Privacy are Key Factors for Artificial Intelligence	117
26	Compliance is Magic!	120
27	Lemmings at the Office	124
28	Kafka and Compliance	127
29	The Performance Zone	130
30	A Yellow Friend	133
31	Virtual Heritage	137
32	Augmented Vision	140
33	Internet of Things – The Gonk Risk	144
34	…and ends.	147
	Bibliography	149
	About the Author	155

INTRODUCTION

"Life is a real-time adventure." The middle of the 1980's saw home computers slowly replacing video consoles in the house-holds. Even if the focus stayed on entertainment, they offered the possibility for "serious" usage. But also the game designers benefited from higher memory and a keyboard. Adventure games became popular, first as text-only games a "Zork"[1] or the "Hitchhiker's Guide to the Galaxy". Later graphics had been added. First single pictures, later point-and-click adventures a la "Manic Mansion" or "Indiana Jones" conquered the screen. Philip K. Dick predicted that life is nothing else than a big computer simulation and for a first time, the idea became understandable.

However you perceive reality, important is to not forget playing with it. Especially when we think about the future, which everyday gets further shaped by scientists and artists. New realities await for established companies, but also the entrepreneurs. As reader of this book you already took the "red pill" and keep asking about tomorrow's wonderland.

Fostering STEM (science, technology, engineering and mathematics) is the new buzzword to discuss raising competitiveness in science and technology. The idea is to present these topics more vividly at school to motivate more pupils to choose related topics later at university. The Talking Heads became famous for progressive pop music, which they combined with artistic videos. For this, it is no surprise that their former front-man David Byrne argued that *"in order to really succeed in whatever... math and the sciences and engineering and things like that, you have to be able to think outside the box, and do creative problem solving... the creative thinking is in the arts."*[2] Arts has be included into the concept (now STEAM) and the schools' timetables. With a further step, educators underline the importance of reading. This as books not only transport information, but furthermore inspire the readers. STREAM explains why business leaders should not only read regarding books and articles, but furthermore science fiction. Many of today's developments had

---

[1] Woyke, Elizabeth (2017): "The Enduring Legacy of Zork"

[2] StarTalk Radio (2017): "The Science of Creativity, with David Byrne"

been described a long time before, and tomorrow's risks and opportunities also already had been addressed.

Welcome to "ACCESS GRANTED: Tomorrow's Business Ethics Vol.2"! In a classic sense you have science fiction in your hands, as it analyzes today's developments to discuss to which potential tomorrow's scenarios they may lead. The different chapters provide answers, and at the same time give the reader new questions to think about. As with all good science fiction, tomorrow's visions are in this or another way already relevant for today. This also as at the end, human- and machine-learning & -behavior is not that different.

A2-1 AND SO IT BEGINS

In a 2013 experiment, Eyal Aharoni and his teams tried to predict the probabilities of prisoners, shortly to be released, to be in prison again inside the next four years. To do so, they took a sample of 96 male prisoners and let them execute computer tasks, which required quick decisions and so triggered impulsive reactions. Situations, where the subjects had no time to think about the consequences of their reactions. While they had been participating in the experiment, the individuals had been connected to a computer to measure the electrical activity of their brains[3] via functional magnetic resonance imaging (fMRI). With this IT-infrastructure, the scientists want to understand if there is statistical relevant relation between the behavior of the brain's anterior cingulate cortex (ACC), responsible for the impulse control, and the probability of a repeated legal violation.

The experiment came to the result that subjects with a relative low ACC-brain activity in the experience had twice the risk to violate the law inside the next four years.[4]

As other experiments confirmed earlier, the human brain develops depending its usage, especially in younger years. So the AAC structure is partly based on what we learnt, we are not born like that.[5]

Furthermore such brain tests does not automatically predict violations of laws and guidelines, but in this case the sample included a populations who already learnt such violations as possible behavior. Accordingly, the individuals could learn other scripts. With this, in a spontaneous situation the subject would not start the earlier script to violate the law, but instead start the new stronger one, to not do it and resist the temptation. Such a

---

[3] Brain Box (2015): "What does fMRI measure?"

[4] Aharoni, Eyal / Vincent, Gina M. / Harenski, Carla L. / Calhoun, Vince D. / Sinnott-Armstrong, Walter / Gazzaniga, Michael, S. / Kiehl, Kent A. (2012): "Neuroprediction of future rearrest"

[5] Henz, Patrick (2017): "Access Granted – Tomorrow's Business Ethics"

new script would have to include not to decide at once, but instead to start a decision making process. Such includes the long-term consequences (returning to prison), but also to build up empathy with the victims.

Due to David Cressey's Fraud Triangle[6], a negative environment may tempt individuals to present a non-proper behavior. In theory, if a risk person enters a risky territory, the overall risk of a legal violation will rise. Today, different networks collect police information, like crimes and their locations to create a real-time public safety map.

The New Inquire Magazine used the idea to create the app (web and iOS) "White Collar Crime Risk Zones". With a special algorithm and machine learning, this app uses information from the Financial Regulatory Authority (FINRA), including financial malfeasance since 1961, with other data as locations of investment advisors, the distribution of liquor licenses and the density of tax-exempt organizations. The result is a real-time map to present the actual white collar crime risk zones inside the United States. Thanks to its data, the software presents also a picture of the potential violator, normally an average age, average looking white male.[7] If the user installed the app on the smart phone, he or she will receive a push-message, when entering in such a danger zone.

Additional cameras, connected to an intelligent software, in the identified risk areas support to understand patterns in movement and behavior which lead later to non-adequate behavior.[8] Such information can confirm the conclusions from the earlier neuropredictions and make this process more adequate. The psychological theories can underlines by statistical data.

> Big Data + Statistical Methods + Logical Theories = Smart Data

---

[6] Cressey, Donald (1973): "Other People's Money: A Study in the Social Psychology of Embezzlement"

[7] Clifton, Brian / Lavigne, Sam / Tseng, Francis (2017): "Predicting Financial Crime: Augmenting the Predictive Policing Arsenal"

[8] Yang, Yuan (2017): "China seeks glimpse of citizens' future with crime-predicting AI"

Due to modern data privacy laws, such as the 2018 EU General Data Protection Regulation[9], it is required that a company is transparent for what purposes the collected information will be used. Due to this, it is not allowed to take information (including from the ACC-tests) from the hiring process and use them later, at least not if the individual does not authorized the organisation to do so. But technically it would be possible to use this information to decide, if the candidate is appropriate for later job functions (and its risk levels) and furthermore receive tailor-made training. Taking the next step, these results could be combined with a real time risk map to predict the actual probability that the individual would break a guideline. As said before, this scenario is limited by local data protection laws.

Future technological possibilities make it imperative today to start the discussion about ethical consequences. We want avoid to hire an innocent person based on his brain waves, as they may predict a higher possibility of non-adequate behavior in stress situations, as such would have relevant negative consequences for the organization, or we believe in in the human and the principle that everyone is innocent until a crime could be proven? Furthermore as the last is predicted and not even committed. In fact we do not even have to start the discussion, as the author Philip K. Dick did this for us already in his 1956 short story "The Minority Report".[10]

---

[9] EUGDPR (2017): GDPR Portal

[10] Dick, Philip K. (1956): "The Minority Report"

A2-2 WHIZ KIDS

The implementation of new media always got accompanied by the fear that it would produce a negative impact especially on the younger generation. Similar happened with TV, the first video-consoles, home computers, internet and smart phones. The actual Generation Y (including the Millennials) and Z are digital natives. Since their first steps, they are accustomed to have touch-screens and information around. As parents use tablets and smart phones to calm down their toddlers, they learnt early to use such devices and even get confused if they cannot change the channels on TV with the same whishing movements.

All actual studies confirm that Millennials have strong values and expect such also from their potential employers. In opposite to the 80s' YUPPIES (Young Urban Professionals), salary lost parts of its importance. This as status symbols changed. Expensive cars and apartments lost on importance, but in opposite fast internet connections and virtual acknowledgment, via social media and blogs, gained relevace. In his study "Growing Up Digital", Tap Tapscott concludes that these generations are *"smarter, quicker and more tolerant of diversity than their predecessors."*[11]

So far, good news for companies and their Ethics & Compliance departments. But there is one down side about Millennials, their respect to data privacy and content copyrights is significant lower than at anterior generations. Their different socialization explains it.

---

[11] The Economist (2017): "The kids are alright"

Second Hand Shop, Aachen, Germany

Products are more than their tangible part, but include also an emotional universe. This is today not only relevant for industrial designers, but especially for the developers of digital content. More and more music, books, videos and software are not bought anymore in a physical store, but directly downloaded to computer, MP3-player, mobile phone, eBook reader or TV. As in the past a detailed user manual or artistic cover had been part of the complete package, the consumer had something in their hands to conclude from this to the quality & value of the intangible content as music, video or software. As this is missing now in many cases, people lose the respect for the product and piracy is often perceived as a face-less crime, as nothing gets physically stolen, just additional copies elaborated.[12]

Millennials show a similar mentality also for their own information, as they present often their whole life on Facebook, Instagram, blogs and/or Snapchat. An ideal source for social engineers or cognitive hackers to prepare their attacks.

---

[12] Henz, Patrick (2016): Business Philosophy according to Enzo Ferrari"

As Millennials put more emphasis on their values as on the ruling law, the Ethic & Compliance department has to use a different strategy to reach these young employees, this cannot only be the usage of different media, but also has to include tailor made content. Data Privacy is a relevant topic for the Compliance Officer, as attackers became smarter and employees' attitude to freedom and access to information may be different as defined in ruling law, even if this does not mean that Millennials are not concerned about the protection of information. The IT-infrastructure gets more sophisticated and more and more, the human employee is identified as the weak brick inside the firewall. So it is no surprise that the known hacker Billy Hoffman wants to break with the typical cliché that hackers are nerds spending nights staring at source-codes and are surrounded by empty pizza boxes.[13] In opposite to this picture, hacking has less do to with pure computer skills, but more with work, as an attack requires a high level of preparation, meaning collecting and interpretation of information. This can be done by the hacker itself, but also get automated. "Crawling software" can autonomously search for personal data and AI starts to connect such information from different searches, as for example an LinkedIn profile with company communication and private email-groups. Then on the next step such an intelligent app can understand how different employees are connected in organization and hierarchy.

But this is only one half of the work, to conduct the attack, the hacker has to understand the victim. If it is directly related to the IT infrastructure, its structures must be known. If this is a cognitive attack, as a phishing attack, the hacker must be aware how the human brain works, especially under pressure. Thanks to this, effective cognitive attacks function based on human nature, not only using authority- and time-pressure, but also can play with curiosity and the inner pressure to help people in need.

As organizations are identified the danger, it is up to them to make their employees smarter about data protection, what includes workshop to raise their awareness. At the end, the human brain is nothing more than a super-computer that may be vulnerable to Trojan viruses, which try to pretend a situation of emergency and so trigger a non-adequate behavior. Such can

---

[13] Hoffman, Billy (2017): "Hacking as Cognitive Skills"

include a by-passing of internal guidelines such as click on unknown attached files or chance bank accounts.

Patrick Henz

A2-3 MORE TROUBLE WITH BUBBLES

Newspapers as the Washington Post had been already called obsolete by the 45th US president Donald Trump. But the swan song may come premature, as the old honorable press is analyzing how Artificial Intelligence may raise productivity and revenues.

Amazon's Jeff Bezos bought the Washington Post in 2013 with the promise to not intervene with the newspaper's editors, but leave the paper independent. So far, he kept his promise and the Post is on the way to keep up with the times. In 2016 debuted "Heliograf" an new software which supports the automatization of articles. The software can connect to data bases and take results, as for example from elections and sport events. This works not autonomous, but the journalist hast to feed Heliograf with narrative templates and key phrases. Due to this, the automated articles still feature the journalist's individual style. Doing so, today's mission for Heliograf is not to replace the human employees, but ensure an effective usage for them. Today's world creates every day numerous small events, important for a small number of involved people. They could be locals or also globally distributed. As the public interest is limited, it would not be possible for newspaper to cover each of such events by a human employee. Accordingly to this vision, Heliograf's first job was to cover the first round events at Rio's 2016 Olympics, what the software did without problems. Later in November 2016, it wrote 500 articles with such limited human intervention. That way it created 500,000 clicks on the Post's portal, what is again relevant for the newspaper's revenues.[14] The paper was completely open about its artificial author and, for example, publicized this pro-actively via their Twitter-account "@WPOlympicsbot".[15]

---

[14] Keohane, Joe (2017): "What new-writing bots mean for the future of journalism"

[15] WashPostPR (2016): "The Washington Post experiments with automated storytelling to help power 2016 Rio Olympics coverage"

The newspaper underlined that the software will not change the Washington Post's political attitude or its philosophy. Nevertheless its competitors may push the development further. For the information flow are sender and recipient relevant. Heliograf automatized the sender. A next-generation software may not only connect to information databases but analyze on the other side, the online behavior of the user. Cookies and apps are collection user information, due to this, an intelligent software can create a profile and forecast not only what topics are interested for the individual, but also what he or she wants to read. This based on the idea that the user not only wants to get informed, but also confirm his or her already existing opinions. This makes it possible for the news-portal to create tailor-made articles for every user and each individual would see a different page. Covering different events and even if they would cover the same event, the text would vary.

The individual stays in his or her personal comfort zone and potentially only sees the information and opinion what he or she wants to read. But this avoids the reception of alternative ideas, which could challenge the person to re-think the existing opinion. If the user does not actively seeks information on other news-portals, he or she stays in the existing information bubble. On a higher scale this means that the division of society continuous and the different groups inside the region even may drift farer away.

For populistic governments, this means good news, as a political leader can use *"divide et impera"*. Besides its Latin name, the expression *"divide and rule"* is not based on the Old Romans, but on the Italian philosopher, politician, poet, diplomat and historian Niccolò Machiavelli and his famous book *"Il Principe"* (Italian for "The Prince"), a book about the philosophy of politics and government, especially written for the Medici family, which ruled Firenze and had been the most important family dynasty at this time.[16]

Divide and rule stands for the principle to divide a big group into smaller sub groups, to make them easier to rain. This not just through pure dividing, but also a construction that the new sub-groups are not having

---

[16] Machiavelli, Niccolò (1513): "Il Principe"

relations with each other, but the relations are limited to the one leader. A strategy, what was not Machiavelli's invitation, in fact he received the inspiration for this by the foreign politics of the Roman Empire, already used by Emperor Cesar himself.

Stephen Hawking once said *"The greatest enemy of knowledge is not ignorance, it is the illusion of knowledge."* Due to bubbles, the users receive biased information. Often without being aware of, only "one side of the medal" gets perceived. As the individual does not know that information is missing, he or she falsely assume that everything is transparent and based on this, make his or her decision.

A2-4 CRESSEY 4.0

To reach their goal to enter the protected network, hackers are searching for the weakest brick in the wall. Due to this, most modern attacks are not done by autonomous software, but "cognitive hacks". These are semi-automated attacks, mostly known as "phishing emails", where the hackers want the user to convince to visit a link or directly open an attachment. Of course, webpages or attachments are not what they pretend to be, but the user gives his or her bank information to an unauthorized person or directly activates a dangerous virus.

Apart from this illegal practices, computers and persuasion also exist in the grey area called "Captology". The term is based on Stanford University scientist B.J. Fogg, who started to investigate a type of software, what tries to persuade its users to show certain desired actions. Today the university has a own laboratory dedicated to Captoloy.[17]

The technique follows the rules of cognitive learning, as the user receives for each desired behavior an award. But in opposite to the original experiments, such awards are mostly virtual without a direct value, such as likes or virtual contacts. The GPS community "Waze" works like this, as with each reported traffic jam, the user receives points and small awards, which can include different car designs on the map.

Other Captology strategies include that the user does not have to click actively to start something, but has to do something to stop the process. Streaming platforms as "Netflix" feature an autorun-function, what (if not deactivated in the preferences), let the next episode of the series start automatically.[18]

---

[17] Stanford University (fetched 22.05.2017): "Stanford Persuasive Tech Lab"

[18] Stoecker, Christian (2017): "Werden Sie Teil der Maschine"

Based on "Gamification"-approach, apps can motivate the user to keep in the process. This with telling him or her how much is still missing to stay on the current level or approach to the next one. Activision included such rewards in their 80s video games for the Atari system. For example, after completing five rounds in "Enduro" or reaching 20,000 points in "Pitfall", you could take a photo of the screenshots and send it via letter to the local Activision publisher. With this, the company sent you badge, a worthy trophy to present to your friends! A similar approach is used by "Uber". If drivers want to quit for the day, the app automatically advised how much is missing to reach the desired daily salary or even to achieve a higher. Often such messages motivate the user to continue for one or two drives more. Of course the users profits from change of behavior, but on the other hand, this can go on the costs of social contacts, as family life. Subconsciously, the user gets "bribed", as the app tries that the human violates the original work-life-balance. Such based on a classic management approach as: *"You can't manage people. You can bribe 'em"*.[19]

As both, Cognitive Hacks and Captology want to manipulate the user to bypass internal guidelines, attitudes or even values, they are understood as temptations. Similar as Donald Cressey already defined in its famous "Fraud Triangle".[20]

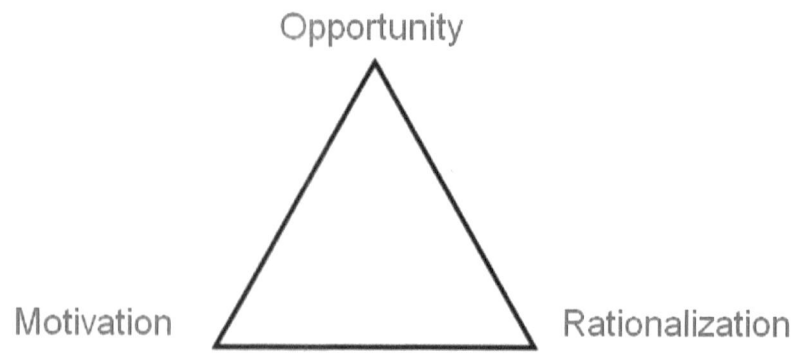

---

[19] Iverson, Kenneth (1998)

[20] Crassey, Donald (1973): "Other People's Money: A Study in the Social Psychology of Embezzlement"

The opportunity is a temptation to "act without thinking". The software pretends to know what is in the user's best interest and offers an easy solution to stay in the personal comfort zone. A critical development, as machines can drag humans into their world, as they try to deactivate or limit the decision making process and let them act similar to trained robots.

Such "automated employees" are a risk factor of the company, as they lost temporary their ability to question their-selves and others. Violation of internal guidelines or external laws are relevant risk factor for the organization.

Based on this, data privacy and cyberattacks, are not a pure IT topic, but Compliance is responsible to protect the company and employees. US president Abraham Lincoln once said in his annual message to the Congress from December 1862 that *"we must rise with the occasion."*[21] Spam-filters and anti-virus software cannot protect the employees against phishing emails or non IT-based "social engineering". Therefor training and workshops are required to foster the individual's knowledge and motivate him or her to not blindly trust an email or software, but, if possible, take the conversation from the virtual to the real world, as strange information from the email should be verified at least with a telephone-call. Even if it is not a classic topic, based on his or her reputation and experience, the Ethics & Compliance Officer can take the responsibility for the organization & employees.

---

[21] Lincoln, Abraham (1862): "Annual Message to the Congress"

A2-5 IT DIVERSITY

Generation Y (including Millennials) and its successor Generation Z are digital natives. Of course, each individual is different and we have to distinguish between the members of each generation. Even if a person uses tablets since the age of a toddler, this does not mean that he or she will develop into a heavy computer / internet user. For this chapter we will have a look at individuals, who spend big parts of the day before the computer and even inside a virtual reality. Thanks to self-selection, such pupils may study IT related topics at the university and join later an IT department.

For an Ethics & Compliance program, these employees are a new focus group. They may be responsible for IT infrastructure, but also Artificial Intelligence solutions, including software implemented in the organization's products and solutions. One risk factor is that individuals, which spend a relevant time inside the virtual world, may lose the connection to the real one. The internet is global without (or at least only a few) borders. Privacy and property laws are often violated without negative consequences. Stakeholders are known via avatar, user-name or email-address. These internet contacts make it difficult to build up empathy for others. Violation to laws and etiquette stay faceless. The consequences of actions are not learnt in a human / legal environment.

This risk is especially for startup companies relevant, as the business model maybe based on one single app. If this software violates existing laws or at least creates the perception that it would do, it may not get accepted by the potential target group. Not only the potential violation of data privacy is a risk, also competition laws. Often a startup is not completely alone with the business idea, but two or three companies are competing who might first solve the problem and market the solution. Being socialized via video games, software designers are tempted to integrate a defense mechanism into their app. Such could work against governmental control or directly the competitor. It may simulate complying behavior to the government or confuse the competitor.

Time pressure leads to regular long working days. Tough deadlines and fatigue make the individual vulnerable for ethical questionable behavior. Group decisions are often more risky than individual ones. This as nobody feels directly responsible. Especially homogenous groups may get affected by the virus. Independent, if it is in a small or big company, new or already established, diverse groups work more effective, as different realities come together and the various experiences, including different values and attitudes, support the decision making process. It is a natural protection against rushed decisions, as hopefully at least one member of the group presents a high involvement into the topic and ensures an extended decision making process.

A2-6 GAIA

Programmers in the late 1980's experimented with the technical possibilities that machines like the 16 Bit Commodore Amiga offered them. Complex simulations had been the result, one of them SimCity, where the user played the role of a mayor & city planner and, from scratch, could start building up his or her own metropolis. SimCity became an instant success and the developer Maxis started a complete Sims-series. One of these titles already had been published the next year: Sim Earth. This time the user was not responsible for a single city, but instead for the whole evolution; from starting the process until actively influencing it. The simulation is based on James Lovelock's Gaia theory. Roughly, he defines the whole planet similar as one living organism, meaning that all creatures as animals, plants and humans.[22] So changes in the different population influence the development of the whole planet. Based on this, players easily could bring their creation out of the equilibrium and the whole life was doomed.

Much earlier, in 1926 the Serbian-American inventor Nikola Tesla said: *"When wireless is perfectly applied, the whole earth will be converted into a huge brain…"* With this he forecasted today's reality. Important is that brain is not synonym for intelligence. As already experienced with its predecessors, print, radio and television, the usage of medium depends on its users. Even if the internet can connect the individual to the knowledge of the whole civilization, most individuals use it to socialize instead of gaining additional education.

If we use Tesla's idea and understand the connected users as part of one big global brain, it is clear that we as connected group are vulnerable to similar psychological biases as a single person. Depending on the information-input, parts of the group may get pushed outside the their personal comfort-zone, right into the panic-zone. Due to social-media and the high grade of interconnection between the users, especially inside

---

[22] Lovelock, James (1972): "Gaia as seen through the atmosphere"

different interest groups, the individuals infect each other's until most parts are either in the panic or comfort zone. As the first ones are more emotionally involved, there is a high risk that a low number of panicked users may infect the whole group, especially as they would communicate more than the ones in the comfort area. This effect can be actively supported / manipulated by news-portals, as often users regularly return to their favorite portals and avoid visiting others, from which they assume that the present other political opinions.

An example that users infect others comes from way back in time, before internet and even before the TV. In 1898 the English author H.G. Wells publish his novel "The War of the Worlds"[23]. 40 years later Orson Welles took the book and used it as base for a radio drama. At that time, radio was the leading media and enjoyed a high credibility in the US, as all over world. This as reporters spoke from the different locations and brought the, at this time mostly negative news, into the homes of the people sitting around the receiver. Welles produced the radio play similar to such a news show. In the beginning of the transmission it was announced as fictive show of the "Mercury Theatre on the Air", but many listeners joined shortly after and so perceived it as real news instead of fiction. Intelligent life on Mars was a broadly accepted possibility and many people started to panic. With the high stress level, they not tried to confirm the message, while dialing (it was still not common to just push a button to switch from channel to channel) to another station. Instead they called their friends and families and even run to public buildings to warn their neighbors. More and more people panicked and called the local police stations or prepared for the invasion.

As confirmed, similar to an individual, also groups can develop a tunnel-vision. Accordingly the solution. Breaks and the active seeking for outside information allows to get a broader overview over the situation. Even if it is not easy, an effective solution could be to find regular offline time. This way the user steps temporary out of the collective and becomes an autonomous individual, who is dependent on independent thinking. Without relying on others, the person may come to different resolutions and build up an healthy skepticism against the globally published

---

[23] Wells, Herbert George (1898): "The War of the Worlds"

information and opinions.

It can be observed that also intelligent people use a big part of their time watching relative stupid TV-formats or similar pages on the internet. But nevertheless they don't perceive an inner barrier to access also more intellectual sources and so achieve relevant new insights. If the individuals are lacking of adequate education, their inner wall stops them to access the university or library portals. A known phenomena, as for example in Germany, where most universities don't require fees, children from parents with lower educational backgrounds later also statistically don't try to go to university, even if the government would financially support them. So the access to education is no pure financial topic, but depends strongly on the socialization. If this division could not get overcome, the society stays the same or even drifts more far away from each other.

A2-7 CYBERDYNE

In 2017 started the a company to offer an automated contract review based on Artificial Intelligence. The software had been able read, review and understand the legal document. Furthermore it could compare the text with the company's rules and requirements. As the A.I. understood the text, it could include different Compliance provisions, regarding the risk factor of the project.[24] Such flexibility regarding territory, type of end customer, including intermediates, reputation, etc. is especially for Compliance departments interesting. This is only the first step for the software, future versions will be connected to different databases to be automatically up to date with all regulation and furthermore may have access to different risk indicators to autonomously decide what risk related decision are adequate.

With this possibilities is A.I. not only a solution to reduce costs, but the automatization can in addition to this, foster the accuracy of the legal review. Due to Chess Grand Master Dimitri Kasparov this is the last the real advantage of the artificial brain against the human one. If a human is playing on his highest level, the machine cannot beat him or her. But in most of the cases, the individual is not able to keep this level up for the whole time of the match, as he or she gets distracted. This is the moment where the machine uses its advantage to beat the human opponent in the game. Similar to Chess, the legal requirements are complex, but limited and perfectly defined.

The review of legal documents is the ideal field for A.I., but nevertheless companies work also on other functions, as for example a Human resources chat-bot. This A.I. can read and understand a curriculum. The human applicant does not wait until the company would schedule a first call with the individual. But the software can nearly instantly, after receiving the CV, contact the applicant on the computer and tablet, and start a first basic interview. Due to such advanced possibilities, most of the individuals, who

---

[24] Lawgeex.com (fetched 16.05.2017): "features"

had already had been participating inside such an interview, thought to be in contact with a human HR person. After a successful job interview, the A.I. still can provide maps or tips on adequate clothing. Such a bot is not only for the hire process interesting, but could support also the internal selection of candidates, for example for a project team.[25]

As it is valid for a human recruiter, also a A.I. may be affected by a psychological bias: similarity often produces sympathy and a preference for the candidate. This can lead to the scenario that the human applicant will prepare him- or her-self for an interview with machines. This may include the service of another A.I., who optimizes the curriculum and could take the role of a sparring partner to simulate the job interview. Such a machine could explain and demonstrate where a recruiter bot puts its focus and what could make the candidate to appear attractive to progress to the next round, then with the human recruiter.

---

[25] Prior, Ryan (2017): Your next job interview could be with a recruiter bot."

A2-8 DEMING'S WORLD OF TOMORROW

All of his life Walt Disney believed that technological progress would work in the benefit of humanity. Based on this philosophy, he created the *"Carousel of Progress"* for the 1964 New York World's Fair. In this attraction, the visitors can follow a typical US family through the 1900s, '20s, 40s and the 21st century; the last updated in 1993. As the carousel had been one of Disney's favorite creations, he installed it after the World's Fair inside Disneyland, where it stayed open until 1973. Two years later, it reopened in the Tomorrowland area of the Disney's Magic Kingdom. Thanks to its retro futuristic charm, the carousel seems like a ride from another time in opposite to the fast-paced attractions around. But especially because of this, it is a recommendation to visit it inside the park. A romantic view on how technology influenced family life and an inspiration to discuss how it will continue. Not only at home, but also in the work environment, where we spend big parts of our days.

MIT professor William Edwards Deming defined in his book *"The New Economics for Industry, Government, Education"* his theory of the *"System of Profound Knowledge"*, which includes four pillars:

- Appreciation for a system
- Knowledge about variation
- Theory of Knowledge
- Psychology[26]

This approach is based on his diverse background as engineer, statistician and management consultant. Important is that all four points interact with each other and so the sorted mathematical world of the system stands in direct contact with the chaotic human psychology.

---

[26] Deming, William Edwards (2000): "The New Economics for Industry, Governance, Education"

The base is the system, planned by Deming from the supplier via the production assembly up to the consumer. Thanks of the detailed knowledge about systems and all factors that can influence them, we are able to plan and manage it as efficient as possible. Thanks to information and experience, changes inside the process are not randomized, but are based on a theory (where the change should take place, what it provokes and how it would affect the total efficiency) and get measured. To do so, it is not only necessary to forecast the output of the potential change, but have a complete overview, which changes are possible to execute.

The first three pillars are mathematically based and could be interpreted as a dehumanization of the working environment. In opposite to this, Deming's fourth pillar "psychology" underlines the essential importance of the human factor. Similar to philosophers as Ayn Rand, he defines that every employee has the right to find his or her personal happiness through work. To maximize the efficiency of the system, the employer has to remove all barriers which stand against this goal. The human employee is the relevant success factor. With this, Deming became an advocate for the humanization of the system.

As result of his research he came to the conclusion that *"a bad system will beat a good person every time."* A non-adequate process will not lead only to suboptimal overall results, but can also provoke employees to violations (confirming Donald Cressey's Fraud Triangle). This based on instinctive protection against the limitation of personal freedom or as the bureaucracy does not offer sufficient space to act based on personal values.

Even if this model had been elaborated at the end of the last millennium, it can be used to create an adequate work environment where robots, Artificial Intelligence and humans can act together. The individual stands in the focus. Tasks which could get automated, will be done my machines; tasks which require a human, are done by such. As consequence, and defined by Deming, they have to be treated as humans and not machines, which includes the possibility that they can satisfy their psychological and self-fulfillment needs, as defined in "Maslow's Hierarchy of Needs"[27]. The

---

[27] Maslow, Abraham (1943): "A Theory of Human Motivation"

systems is flexible to adapt itself to the different individuals instead that they have to adapt to the processes. Thanks to Industry 4.0, processes get smarter and allow more possibilities for adaption.

Skilled and motivated employees are the key factor for successful and sustainable business. Acting on values is a form of respect, for internal and external stake holders. Being respected means responsibility, as people put their trust in you. A positive reputation is a sales advantage. Acting based on values, and not only guidelines, supports this advantage. To achieve this position, the rules must leave enough space for the heart. This is no contradiction, as guidelines could be designed to include this freedom. Furthermore clear rules can protect the employees, as they can act based on their values inside the defined space. Besides defining the day-by-day business, this complies furthermore with the original vision of the company founder. These pioneers started the organization often with a dream to make a difference in the world, and not only earn money based on their business concept. Artificial Intelligence can support in creating such an adequate system to ensure that the founder's vision gets respected by supporting today's employees with working based on the corporate and personal values.

A company is a decentralized structure. Of course a lot of knowledge is at the top, but experience and intelligence is spread over the complete organizational infrastructure inside the individual employees. Astrophysicist Neil deGrasse Tyson explained that a planet does not technically orbits it host star, but instead bot bodies effectively orbit their common center of mass.[28] This picture explains that all employees are responsible for their radius. Business consultant Ira Chaleff concludes that leadership is not about followers and team-members do not exist to satisfy theirs leader. Instead both are part of the system and responsible for their area of gravity, this to maximize the efficiency of the complete system. As micro-system, the group has not only to fulfill its particular tasks, but also to uphold the company's vision and values. The same applies also for the single employee. To achieve this, all employees require at least a basic knowledge about the company's strategy and business philosophy.

---

[28] deGrasse Tyson, Neil (2017): "Astrophysics for People in a Hurry"

Additional to the *"System of Profound Knowledge"* Deming elaborated the *"14 Points for Management"*[29]. Both concepts use a different approach, but come to comparable results. Here he demands the continuous and constant improvement of the system, as could be ensured by a flexible AI setup and furthermore to drive out any kind of fear. A positive and transparent corporate culture ensures that humans and AI can would together without prejudices.

Such a positive picture is valid for job positions, where human ingenuity and creativity generates an advantage against the robots or software. If this is not given, job positions get automatized. It is the Government's task to prepare society for this development.

---

[29] Deming, William Edwards (1986): "Out the Crisis"

A2-9 ALIEN INSIDE

Director Ridley Scott brought 1979 a movie into the theaters, which should define a new genre. A combination between science fiction and horror, this in dark technological settings. Its status as a cult movie reached *"Alien"*[30] also thanks to the used designs by the Swiss painter and visual artist H.R. Giger. The plot of the movie is fast told. The crew of the commercial spacecraft *"Nostromo"* received an unknown transmission, coming from a planetoid. To investigate this, they landed on the surface and discovered an alien space ship. Inside are numerous eggs. One Alien slipped, attacked and attached to a crew-member. Violating quarantine regulations and disobeying the direct orders by Warrant Officer Ripley, they crew brought the Alien on board. They had been able to de-tach it, but by then it already included its egg inside the incautious Kane. Shortly later a newborn Alien slipped outside his stomach and continuously killed one-by-one the crew members, before finally Ripley could kill it.

Quarantine regulations, the same as all company guidelines, are published to define behavior in certain situations and with this limit the risk for the organization. Inside the defined space, employees can act safely, using their skills and live-out creativity for the benefit of the company. In general, individuals have the wish for a positive self-awareness and due to this, feel the pressure to help, if they perceive another human or living being in need. As this is an emotion, it may block the logical thinking. A potential weakness which may get exploited by rogue employees or external social hackers, which pretend to be in unhappy situation and request the employee to help them out. Based on the individual skills, but bypassing company guidelines, such support is possible for the employee. Based on this schema, individuals fall in such attacks. Results are often a smaller or bigger loss for the organization.

---

[30] Scott, Ridley (1979): "Alien"

Being a good corporate citizen is a defined value for most organizations. The company wants to support altruistic behavior of its employees. To protect them against the earlier mentioned attacks, guidelines have to leave space to act based on the heart without losing safety. Potential processes for emergencies have to be defined. On the other hand, the company shall raise awareness to protect their employees against manipulation. It has to be avoided to let the Alien creature enter the organizational structures.

But it does not always require such a monster to destroy the group. The *"Biosphere 2"* project in the 1990s simulated a closed biosphere without any direct contact to the outside, similar to a potential Martian colony. The experiment should run two years, but the two attempts had to be stopped earlier. The first time due to low oxygen levels inside the biosphere and the second time based on mismanagement until potential sabotage of participating crew members. Even if the original time-limit could not be reached, both attempts gave scientists precious information, as the organizers of a flight to Mars are aware how difficult the mission is related its human factor and where things can start to go wrong.[31]

At the end distinguishing between humans and aliens is not relevant. Astronomy professor Sten Hasselquist of the New Mexico State University explained the results of his study, where he and his team screened more than 150,000 stars: *"The elements we measure include the atoms that make up 97% of the mass of the human body."* These include carbon, hydrogen, nitrogen, oxygen, phosphoron and sulfur.[32] These elements not only exist all over in the known university, but furthermore already at the time of the Big Bang. As US astronomer Carl Sagan said: *"We are made of star stuff".*[33]

---

[31] Mellino, Cole (2016): "The World's Largest Earth Science Experiment: Biosphere 2"

[32] Phys.org (2017): "The elements of life mapped across the Mily Way by SDSS/APOGEE"

[33] Sagan, Carl (1980): "Cosmos"

W. Edwards Deming defined employees as center of the system. [34] This philosophy explains that not only a bad system can negatively influence a good person, but also the individuals itself can do that. A team is more than a group of talented individuals, but they must have a fit to work efficiently together. Extroversive & introversive individuals, conflict-seekers & -avoiders and artists & workers have to perform as one effective team. A diversity of thought and behavior supports such a fit and avoids the development of a "group tunnel-view". Team-skills are not only based on the individual characters, but also are learnt behavior. Linked to company and personal values, working together is a logical derived attitude. Workshops can deliver such a message.

What is true for human employees also have to be applied for Artificial Intelligence. The character of the A.I. has to be adapted to fit not only to the general culture in region, but particularly to the individual user or group. To ensure that individuals build up a trustful working relationship with their AI colleagues, all of them have to be on same level of information. Especially science fiction often draws a picture that the machines follow secret protocols. As in the "Alien"-movie, the android Ash received the secret order to bring one of the eggs back from the mission.

Most common scenario to provoke resistance is change. Humans mostly do not like it, as it brings them out of their individual comfort zones. If they don't understand the need and their personal benefit, reactions can reach from passive resistance to open active and even hidden active resistance, as sabotage. The last include classic actions as the destroying of company property, but thanks to social media can also manifest in anonymous "resistance"-profiles to communicate critical information to the public.

To avoid the such negative effects, the first step is to motivate the employees for the change. Show them how it would positively influence them, so that they actively request the change. In this scenario, it is not a "push-strategy", but the individuals "pull" the change from the company. Second part is to continuously inform the individuals about the different

---

[34] Deming, William Edwards (2000): "The New Economics for Industry, Governance, Education"

steps of the process, with that the employees perceive staying in control and that it will be a change to a known goal instead being an road trip into the uncertain. Nevertheless, even with the best preparation and execution, the risk is that not all employees get reached and leave the company. This can be on purpose or forced as they are not able to comply with the new requirements. Change comes with a cost, but as the evolution thought, missing change may lead to extinction.

A2-10 THE A.I. COACH

The integration of Artificial Intelligence into companies will create complete new job profiles. One of them is the *"AI Compliance Officer"*, but also the "AI Coach".

After AIs already won in Chess and other board games against their human opponents, in 2015 Google let their DeepMind-AI learn different classic Atari games[35], such as *"Ms. Pac Man"*, *"Space Invaders"*, *"Video Pinball"*, *"Q-Bert"* and *"Montezuma's Revenge"*. The AI started with trial-and-error. The software learned based on *"classic conditioning"*, as it received a positive amplifier. This similar to *"Pavlov's Dog"*. In the beginning the AI made only slow progress, but then advanced and at the end could beat the human high scores in Space Invaders and Video Pinball. With the more complex Ms. Pac Man and Montezuma's Revenge the program still struggled.

Around two years later Microsoft changed the setup to *"cognitive learning"*. The AI observed human players and learnt from its mentors. In total the human players created 45 hours of gameplay, which was analyzed by the machine. Nevertheless that the AI still had its problems with Montezuma's Revenge, in average the machine learnt faster from the human players, as it did on its own before. Based on this, Microsoft concluded that with adequate human teachers an AI is learning faster.[36] Just as it applies for humans.

Inside an organization employees may require temporary coaches, as they have the required technical knowledge, but may lack of soft skills. Such raw talents need support by experienced colleagues to reach the next level of their career. A possible solution is to team them up with a higher manager, who acts as a coach, so that he / she can learn the required skills, such as emotional intelligence. Cognitive learning is used.

---

[35] Cooper, Daniel (2015): "Google's newest AI can beat your Atari highs-scores"

[36] Dent, Steve (2017): "Humans can help AI learn games more quickly"

Similar to this scenario, special coaches may teach AI software to make the adequate decisions. This is relevant as decisions not only have to be maximized for the short-term, but to ensure sustainability to maximize the long-term profit. Ethics & Compliance have to be obeyed, even if impunity would not punish violations to law. The AI has to understand that nevertheless there is a cost of corruption, which can manifest itself, for example, in shrinking markets, raising costs and low profit margins. Even fines based on global investigations have to be considered. Business decisions have to be based on law and values. Furthermore, the AI have to fit to internal organization, including to the human employees. Based on region or even group culture, the software has to interact differently with its human colleagues. Human and machine diversity are no single topics, but the human machine group requires such.

Human AI Coaches can teach such ethical decision making to ensure that the algorithm mathematically understands that transparent business ensures long-term success, even if on the short-term this may lead to lower results. As each company has its individual Code of Conduct, mostly based on its founder, decision making has its individual variations, so that the machines could not learn such behavior automatically from similar software used in different companies. Trail-and-error can easily lead to high fines and reputational damage, cognitive learning and "human understanding" is the more effective solution.

Today's Compliance Officers claim that ethical behavior leads to sustainability and is a sales advantage. The vision has to be expressed in mathematical formulas and show a higher expected value than the output of corrupt behavior. If this is not possible to explain, not the AI, nor human employees will understand the message.

Microsoft's Maluuba AI was a good student and reached in Ms. Pac Man the perfect score of 999,999 points, more than every human player reached in history.

ACCESS GRANTED Vol.2: Tomorrow's Business Ethics

A2-11 COMPLIANCE NEW DEFINED

"Disruption" is in fashion today, to stop the current and give opportunity to the new. Disruption does not automatically mean that something will be implemented, but that a break can be used to think about the status quo and potential alternatives. A new decision making process will choose between continuing on the known path or change to a new one.

For an individual regular disruptions are required to avoid a "tunnel vision" and related behavior risks. In our modern times it gets more and more complicated to get a break, as thanks to connected smart devices employees read and answer their emails not only inside their regular working hours, but also before and after, including on week-ends and holidays. Even the classic TV-evening does not give the required escape, as tablet and smart phones became a regular "second screen" to switch the eyes between TV and computer.

Important possibility for disruption are the employee's holidays or also business travels. "Traveling educates" is not only a phrase, but new locations and meeting other people are always a source of inspiration. The individual connects the new impression with his or her actual life and tasks. After the time off, such new ideas can make the person re-think his or her tasks and, hopefully, make such more effective.

Cuedzalan, Puebla, Mexico

The company's HR department shall ensure that employees take their annual holidays and furthermore that over-time gets limited. Employees with a "private life" receive input from different settings. Inspirations and fresh ideas get back to the company and due to this, the employee gets more valuable for the organization. Bill Gates understood this relation and once said: *"I choose a lazy person to do a hard job. Because a lazy person will find an easy way to do it."* He formulated it provocative, because being outside the office does not mean being lazy, as leisure time can be used actively.

Especially today, where jobs get automatized by robots and AI, the company shall be aware that on positions where we need human employees, we have to treat them as such and not similar to machines. If not, humans are vulnerable for failures and errors. Humans treated as humans, develop the skills to protect themselves against negative psychological biases.

Disruption is relevant for all corporate functions. The Compliance department is still a relative new function, implemented as reaction to big corporate scandals or new legal requirements. It had been added to already existing organizational functions. Now it is a good time to take a break and analyze if this setup is the best fit, or if we want to have something else.

William Edwards Deming started as an electrical engineer who specialized later in mathematical physics, before he became a management consultant. Based on his background he took a different view on organizational structures and elaborated his *"System of Profound Knowledge"*, including the four pillars:
- Appreciation for a system
- Knowledge about variation
- Theory of Knowledge
- Psychology[37]

To ensure an efficient change management, Deming first had to convince his clients that his systematical approach had been adequate and brought a fresh insight. He presented all different company functions from procurement to sales as one big system, where the different parts interact with each other, including with external stakeholders. Deming's clients understood and appreciated this systematical approach. After this he could analyze the different available options and how the variation of decisions could lead to higher or lower efficiency level of the whole system. This required expert knowledge to forecast the outcome. The idea was to use cognitive learning instead a simple trail-and-error-approach. Based on his research, Deming concluded that the employees are part of the system, but playing an outstanding role.

In his later role as business consultant for Toyota he implemented this concept in 2001, known as *"The Toyota Way"*. The two pillars included "Continuous Improvement" and "Respect for People". This is not only a symbiosis of US and Japanese philosophy, but can be identified in all time and cultures as base for business success. Already decades earlier Enzo Ferrari defined the company's output as result of effective teamwork: *"What we do here is elite work."*[38]

---

[37] W. Edwards Deming (1986): "Out of the Crisis"

[38] Henz, Patrick (2017): "Business Philosophy according to Enzo Ferrari"

Based on his psychological knowledge, Deming recognized that a non-efficient infrastructure, a bureaucratic burden, has a negative impact on the employees. Taking Donald Cressey's Fraud Triangle[39] into consideration, bureaucracy is a temptation to bypass it, especially if its benefit is not understandable. Due to this, the organizational setup (physical location, tools, processes, guidelines, company values) must be created to support the employees and not the other way around. This philosophy is aligned with the concept of Industry 4.0, where automatization adapts to the user and not the human employee to the machines, as still in Industry 3.0

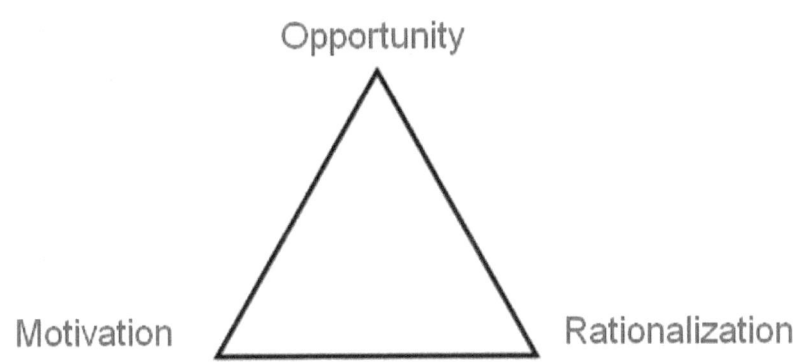

Based on a systematical approach, what triggers compliance with internal guidelines and external laws? *"Information"*. Information what is the adequate behavior, what is the content of the relevant guidelines and what is the potential result of the behavior (likelihood and impact, including for "getting caught with violation a law of guideline"). The cost of corruption has to be understood by the individual, before he or she can develop empathy for the victims. Based on this, Compliance has to reduce the costs to gain information, for example by being close to the business.

Information is the critical resource for businesses and organizations, as they require access and ownership of such. Information is mandatory for successful companies and its value is on the raise. So it is no surprise that information becomes even jewelry. The US Rosetta Project seeks via

---

[39] Crassey, David (1973): "Other People's Money: A Study in the Social Psychology of Embezzlement"

crowd-funding to finance its first prototype of long-term archive. The only three inch diameter nickel disk should store 14,000 pages of information. Similar to the famous Rosetta Stone, it should include over 1,000 languages to store them for the next thousands of years. The production of numerous disks should ensure that at least a few of them survive the centuries.[40] The small size makes the Rosetta Disk an ideal object to create necklace or other piece of art or jewelry.[41] Another example is "FrontRow" from Uniquiti Labs, a camera for livestream in the form of a necklace. Thanks to its operation system, the device can send the videos automatically to Facebook or a blog.[42]

The problem with information is not only a potential missing access to it, also the opposite: the overflow caused by numerous news portals and social platforms makes it impossible for humans to timely analyze information. Specialized providers and AI software may get used to summarize the daily articles and decide which are relevant and which not. As perceptional biases always exist, it is the question, how reliable are such services, especially if a computer should decide what is relevant for humans.[43] Trust is needed, especially if the success of the company depends on this information. Such providers have to be auditable.

Reality is not the same for people, in fact, each individual builds its own reality, based on information and the perception of information. In George Orwell's classic "1984" the characters Winston and O'Brien discussed if the past exists. In the beginning of the dialogue it is clear: *"In records. It is written down."*[44] A logical definition, as we think to know our past, as it is documented in history books. Sometimes a false perceived safety, as books only represent the actual status of history. Theories exist until they get dis-

---

[40] The Rosetta Project (fetched 21.06.2017)

[41] Sayej, Nadja (2017): "This Old School Wearable Puts a Thousand Languages Around Your Neck"

[42] Lazzaro, Sage (2017): "Look, no hands! $399 camera necklace lets you livestream videos directly to Facebook, Instagram, and YouTube without lifting a finger"

[43] Knight, Will (2017): "An Algorithm Summarizes Lengthy Text Surprisingly Well"

[44] Orwell, George (1949): "1984"

confirmed. Also history books have to be rewritten, when archeologists find new clues and evidence. The more a thesis gets communicated, the more believable it sounds. Especially when it comes from different sources, which gets perceived as independent. This applies for correct and false information. Relevant is that new information gets perceived based on the already existing experience. Similar to using glasses, personal believes frame the perception of new information. It is a logical conclusion for Orwell's character: *"reality is not external and only exists in the human mind, and nowhere else."*[45] Each new information gets perceived through the glasses of existing information. But furthermore, with this it changes slowly the individual's inner reality. If information gets erased from books, websites, and other alternative information communicated, the original reality will become unreal for the perceiver; later forgotten and replaced by the new message. In other words, it is *"the abolition of the past".*[46] This effect can be used for the good and bad. If a corporation wants to implement a relevant change, it should work with repeated messages to present a vision of the new reality. With the repeating, employees will perceive it as relevant and the existing perceived reality slowly gets understood as a status which has to be changed.

Joshua Hartshorne suggested to think about the way that language frames thoughts: *"words are very handy mnemonics. We may not remember what seventeen spools looks like, but we can remember the word seventeen."*[47] The English language distinguishes between "accountability" and "responsibility":

- Accountability: *"In ethics and governance, accountability is answerability, blameworthiness, liability, and the expectation of account-giving."*[48]
- Responsibility: *"Responsibility may refer to: being in charge, being the owner of task or event."*[49]

---

[45] Orwell, George (1949): "1984"

[46] Mohomed, Carimo (2011): "The abolition of the Past: History in George Orwell's 1984"

[47] Hartshorne, Joshua (2009): "Does Language Shape What We Think?"

[48] Diffen (fetched 16.11.2017): "Accountability vs. Responsibility"

[49] Diffen (fetched 16.11.2017): "Accountability vs. Responsibility"

"Accountability" is stronger than "responsibility", as it includes the individual's perception of ownership.[50] Roman languages, however, do not define this difference. Less precise they translate "accountability" as the weaker "responsibility" (Italian: "responsabilità", Portuguese: "responsabilidade", Spanish: "responsabilidad"). This indicates a risk that target groups from these countries are less familiar with the concept of "accountability". For Ethics & Compliance communication and workshops this means that it had to be ensured that texts with the two words get adequately translated, and if a training speaks about responsibility and / or accountability, the facilitator has to explain the specific differences.

Besides the language barrier, chat-bots infuse new risks into the transportation of information. In- and outside the corporation the creation and communication of information gets automatized. In general, this supports a higher level of quality, as even specialized documents and articles get sent to the right target group. But again, as all connected software, they are vulnerable against hacker-attacks, biases and viruses. If this is the case they can sabotage the information-flow by shutting down the service or the creation and transportation of wrong information.

Even if reality only exists inside the individual, organizations have to ensure that at least these realities get similar. This can get reached by using adequate ("real") information from "objective" sources. The better the input of information, the better also the results of the decision making process. This applies for human and artificial intelligence.

Based on this idea, Compliance hast to ensure transparency and minimize the costs to gain reliable information. Raising levels of misinformation (including perceptional bias) are a Compliance risk, as it leads to non-adequate behavior.

If we set the focus on "information", it is logical that the Compliance department is not only responsible for human employees, but also to foster data privacy and cybersecurity. Adequate behavior requires transparent information, as behavior is based on information. This is true for human

---

[50] YouTube (2009): "Responsibility vs Accountability"

employees and Artificial Intelligence. Amazon CEO Jeff Bezos said in 2017 that A.I. is in its golden age. The first companies already implemented such intelligent software and all others will follow in the next months and years. Human employees and AI have both to follow the rules and guidelines. Compliance is an established function to do this for humans, so it is a natural evolution that the department will take on this responsibility also for AI.

Traditional computer security has the goal to protect against autonomous attacks. Understanding how the IT protection of an organization works, most hackers identified the human employee as the weak brick inside the firewall. As result, most of today's cyberattacks are based on cognitive hacking. This strategy is dangerous, as the hackers not only know how the computer works, but also how the brain does. The attacks take advantage of the different psychological biases, as for example obedience to authority or on the other hand the wish to help people in need. Similar to situations in the "real world", such cognitive hacks can lead to "ethical blindness" and related non-adequate behavior, such as violating of guidelines and corruption. Just as a Trojan Virus, the misinformation gets into the human brain and delude the individual a different reality to trigger a non-adequate behavior.

At the end is the human brain nothing else a super-computer and the protection of both, human and computer, is similar. Inspired by the "Framework of Improving Critical Infrastructure Cybersecurity", an Integrity Program can be described with Identify, Protect, Detect, Respond and Recover.[51]

Even if the focus of the Integrity of Information (IoI)-program would be on "Protect", the heart is on "Detect". Efficient controls not only ensure transparency, and is a required process to win information, but furthermore create respect for the Integrity Officer (IO). To ensure this, the processes and controls shall be as bureaucratic as required to be as strong as possible. To reach this, a continuous review of its guidelines, tools and controls is

---

[51] National Institute of Standards and Technology (2014): "Framework for Improving Critical Infrastructure Cybersecurity"

part of the "Protect"-pillar. As even the strongest control system cannot detect every violation on time, an anonymous whistleblower hotline is a mandatory add-on and of course, its effective, control. If required, investigations have to gather needed information.

The day-by-day IoI-tasks are related to "Protect" and minimize potential findings in the third pillar. The IO can reach this with being near to the business and organize relevant trainings and workshops with the employees. In these events, required information gets interchanged so that both side understand the other. The information access is relevant inside the organization, so cannot be reduced to personal meetings, as the chance for such a limited. The classic additional option is one-way communication, such as flyers, posters or even newsletters. Artificial Intelligence is offering new ways. Chat-bots can provide a first service level. The employee has the possibility to get answers to his or her frequent levels, even without that the IO gets aware of this missing of knowledge. An important point for cultures, where the "loss of the face" is a relevant factor.

Information is the base of decisions and the company's most important asset. Non-complete or even altered information lead to wrong decisions, even violation of law and guidelines.

Based on this philosophy, Compliance is a service department and friendliness a must. But to earn respect, this is not enough, Compliance must prove that they are able to ensure guidelines and if necessary, execute adequate disciplinary sanctions. As Al Capone once said: *"Don't mistake my kindness for weakness."* If Compliance has this ability to implement such sanctions, employees understand that nobody is above the company guidelines and may overcome the fear to report possible wrongdoing. The absence of impunity motivates employees to play by the rules and demand this from their colleagues, but also management.

The Integrity of Information system includes five pillars, designed around their central one "Detect".

- Identify: Not only each company, but each location and department is different. A regular Integrity Risk Assessment is mandatory to efficiently protect the organization. It identifies the risk factors and the required follow-up actions.
- Protect: If the organization is not in actual problems the focus shall be to stay in this situation. Transparency of Information shall be fostered, employees receive the information they need based on their job position. Tailor-made communication avoids an information-overflow and so the situation that the individual rejects information or would not be able to perceive it.
- Detect: The traditional heart of the Integrity System. The controls should not only detect direct violations, but in general create transparency if the processes are effective, including the preventive measures.
- Respond: "Tone from the Top" is the base for Integrity, as nobody can be above the internal guidelines. Due to this, if a violation gets detected, the response must be adequate, related to the action and not the level of the person.
- Recover: Violations affect the corporate culture up to damaging reputation and causing financial damage. Even the best Integrity Programs cannot guarantee 100% protection, so different scripts have to be prepared how to react in a potential corruption case to limit the reputational damage and finally recover integrity.

As Agent Smith said in the Matrix: *"Never send a human to do a machine's job."* Under ideal conditions, human employees can decide on the same quality level as AI. But in opposite to machines, they do not consistently work at their highest levels, but are influenced by mood, distraction, health and other factors. AI is superior for rule-based tasks. The human strength is creativity and the flexibility to adapt and react to different scenarios. To strengthen the human workforce, the company has to treat them as such. Tasks which are possible to delegate to machines. Compliance messages should inspire and make people think. Humans remember more efficiently, if the information is the result of a thinking-process. Based on this, the

Compliance idea should not always makes it too easy for the employee, but provoke them to think, how to understand it. For example, if an employee has a question for the Compliance Officer, he or she should not directly answer, but send the question back to the employee to solve it on his or her own. As Compliance in most cases is based on common sense, the answer will be correct. The Compliance Officer can confirm this or if required, explain the employee where he or she went wrong.

The learning theory is based on learnt situations, which triggers to execute a learnt behavior, as this leads with a high possibility to a motivator, which satisfies the need. For example, a sales employee needs to pay its open bills, and bribes a procurement person of the client organization. With this he reaches a higher bonus to pay the personal bills. This situation not only applies for objective needs, but also subjective temptations, as the more expensive car or luxury vacations. If the used behavior leads to regular success, the employee will most probably continue with it. Further this extrinsic motivation gets replaced by an intrinsic one. The external motivator is not required anymore to trigger the corrupt behavior. The employee enjoys the flow-experience of bypassing internal process and external laws. Thanks to the ignoring of rules, life gets easier for him or her, a certain feeling of liberty or even superiority gets perceived. As the external amplifier is not required, the corrupt behavior gets shown also in situations with a only minimal benefit. This explains why repeatedly high level employees get caught in small crimes, where the risk of jeopardizing a long business career does not stand in any relation to the potential benefit of violating internal guidelines. Depending on the individual character and the case where such behavior not got caught & sanctioned in the past, employees may underestimate the risk of getting caught. This is an opportunity for the Compliance system, as suspicious behavior can get caught in the regular random samples to control the approval- and control-processes, as for example in sponsoring and donation or the travel expenses. Mafia gangster Al Capone was imprisoned in 1931, not for murder, money-laundry, kidnapping or similar, but tax evasion. First he spent his time in the Federal Prison of Atlanta, before he got transferred to Alcatraz, the prison island in the Bay of San Francisco. 1939 he could leave based on his good behavior.⁵²

Alcatraz, San Francisco

To avoid that a flow-experience even starts, the organization has to establish a clear "0 tolerance"-culture. This not only regarding potential violations of Compliance processes, but all guidelines.

If we take now a moment of disruption, we may come to the conclusion that the actual Compliance setup is understandable based on history, as many corporations implemented it to manage the risk coming from existing anti-corruption laws or even as answer to an actual case.

The authors Nicolas Racz, Edgar Weippl and Andreas Seufert defined a different model, an integrated vision of Governance, Risk and Compliance (GRC). A holistic approach, where the three functions enter their specific responsibilities:⁵³

- Governance ensures that the company has the required guidelines and tools implemented. They must be as strong as necessary to answer to a given risk or opportunity, but on the other hand as non-bureaucratic as possible. The processes must be transparent, and willingly violations sanctioned. Of course processes have to be adequately communicated. This not only includes the elaboration of the guideline itself, but also communication and training. The

---

⁵² Henz, Patrick (2017): "Compliance is a Race Car."

⁵³ Racz, Niclas / Weippl, Edgar / Seufert, Andreas (2010): A Frame of Reference for Research of Integrated Governance, Risk and Compliance (GRC)

process-owner has to be aware of his or her responsibility to foster compliance with the document.
- Risk: Guidelines and processes are no self-purpose, but related to specific risks and opportunities. If such not exist (anymore), there is no reason for a guideline to carry on. It is management's decision, how high the organization's appetite for risk is. This based on its oversight of adequate information. Guidelines document this decision, what concludes employees' duty to comply.
- In opposite to Governance, where the focus is to comply with adequate internal guidelines, Compliance concentrates on external laws, especially based on antitrust, anti-corruption and money-laundry.

The three areas create a triangle, which includes strategy, processes, people and technology. The last two are especially in the process of disruption. For example, the values and attitudes of millennials have become a bigger part of today's workforce. On the technology side, Industry 4.0 and Artificial Intelligence offer fascinating opportunities, but also new risks. Machines may work more effectively than humans, but they also suffer from biases and data protection risks. Today people and technologies change processes and strategies. The model does not mean that GRC is responsible for these four areas, but GRC has to interact with their respective owners.

The 2016 movie "Arrival"[54] (based on the 1998 short story "The Story of Life" by Ted Chiang[55]) presented twelve UFOs arriving on Earth. The alien lifeforms, the "Heptapods", had a different kind of communication, circle-like expressions, with no end and no beginning. This as the culture existed outside a linear timeline. Past, present and future had been known, as they existed in parallel. Such an understanding would mean that framing effects do not exist, as everything gets perceived the same time. For the GRC triangle this would be for benefit, as the function has the temptation to be interpreted based from which angle you perceive it. When GRC evolves

---

[54] Villeneuve, Denis (2016): "Arrival"

[55] Chiang, Ted (1998): "The Story of Life"

from Risk Management, often it will be perceived as an extended version from such. Similar when it starts from the Governance function. For a Compliance Officer taking on the GRC role, it might be different, as Compliance normally works with values and guidelines, already has inside its core function a holistic approach, so would be open to the additional tasks. If GRC gets implemented into a complete new company, the starting point would be the risk assessment. Here the risks & opportunities get identified and top management has to decide which level of risk appetite the new-born organization shall live out. If GRC gets introduced into an existing company, most properly risk management, governance and compliance already exist. Similar to the Heptapods' language, the three points create a triangle, no beginning no end. The new responsible has to define the new function or department, addressing all three angles in parallel.

With ensuring clear structures inside an organization, GRC ensures understandable rules. It protects the employees, if they play inside these rules. Employer and employee trust each other, what both understand as sign of mutable respect.

Patrick Henz

A2-12 CATHARSIS

The Greek word "Catharsis" can be translated with "Cleaning". At the end of the 19th Century the noun was introduced into the world of psychology. With "Catharsis" the scientists defined the potential effect that with living out aggression, for example in boxing or other sports, the individual can reduce its negative emotions. First studies confirmed the theory, but later in the 60' to 80's most studies came to the opposite result that Catharsis fosters aggressive behavior.

In the middle of the 80's the theory made it a last time into the focus of discussion, as experts argued about the effects of warlike computer games, especially as they mostly got played by children and youth. Game publishers argued with the catharsis-theory and politicians often held the learning-theories against that, as the users of such games learned aggression as an accepted behavior leading to a positive result. At the end, both theories could not convince, as video games still not had realistic graphics and the low-pixel animations could not get perceived as human beings by the players. Further studies came to the conclusion that warlike games could foster aggressive behavior, if other negative circumstances are given, as non-functional family structures or peer pressures. Some countries as Germany took consequences and set several titles on an index, so that only adults had been able to buy them. Furthermore, advertising for these games had been forbidden.

Today experts confirm that video games can have a positive effect on children, as reflexes get fostered. Gamification bets on the power of transporting information while playing. With the raise of Augmented and Virtual Reality we have to come back to the learning effects.

The US-author Daniel F. Galouye published in 1964 the novel *"Simulacron-3"*[56], the first book describing Virtual Reality. A company developed a super-computer, which is able to simulate a whole city, until the smallest

---

[56] Galouye, Daniel F. (1964): "Simulacron-3"

detail. Via VT humans could temporary stayed in this second reality. Similar as in *"Total Recall"*[57], users of such virtual worlds have the possibility to take on different roles, including having super-powers. Also it is a safe environment to live out aggressive behavior. In opposite to '80s video games, today's VT comes close to reality. The more real and virtual worlds blur and mix, the higher the chance that learnt behavior in the one world could get used in the other one. What is valid for the good, is a risk for the bad. If players stay a longer time in a perceived as real 1930 Chicago simulation with intact Mafia structures and corrupt politicians, corruption may get learnt as adequate and successful behavior. If individuals are not able anymore to distinguish between virtuality and reality, learnt behavior will be applied in both. A special risk for Augmented Virtuality, where artificial and real individuals act together in the same space. A virtual Pokémon can be treated differently than a real-life dog.

---

[57] Dick, Philip K. (1966): "Total Recall"

A2-13 MACHIAVELLI FOR A.I.

Besides its Latin name *"divide et impera"*, the expression *"divide and rule"* is not based on the Old Romans, but on the Italian philosopher, politician, poet, diplomat and historian Niccolò Machiavelli and his famous book *"Il Principe"* (Italian for "The Prince"), a book about the philosophy of politics and government, especially written for the Medici family, which ruled Firenze and had been the most important family dynasty at this time.[58]

Divide and rule stands for the principle to divide a big group into smaller sub groups, to make them easier to rain. This not just through pure dividing, but also a construction that the new sub-groups are not having relations with each other, but the relations are limited to the one leader. A strategy, what was not Machiavelli's invitation, in fact he received the inspiration for this by the foreign politics of the Roman Empire, already used by Emperor Cesar himself.

Nearly 500 years later this principle gets used for Artificial Intelligence and its learning process. Developers at the Microsoft company Maluu used this concept to teach their AI playing Ms. Pac Man. The software divides the different tasks into sub-tasks:

- Eat energy pills
- Eat the additional fruits
- Escaping the ghosts
- Catching the blue ghosts

As the AI (similar to traditional software) is able to multitask, it calculates for each sub-tasks its own learning algorithm, including virtual positive multiplier for successful executed sub-tasks (as eating an energy pill).[59]

---

[58] Machiavelli, Niccolò (ca. 1543): "The Prince"

[59] Simonite, Tom (2017): "Microsoft Masters Ms. Pac-Man with a Horde of AI Agents"

The four sub-tasks work simultaneously, but completely independent from each other. The AI takes the average value as the direction for Ms. Pac Man. Just as Machiavelli defined, the AI separated the four sub-tasks and then evaluated on the next higher level the results to merge them into the decision in which direction Ms. Pac Man should move.

In times where we became Cyborgs, as part of our memory was outsourced to Wikipedia and other parts of the internet, we can analyze how machine learning may get used for humans, too. Companies are in the process to go find new paths for their training, and "micro-learnings" is one of them. Instead to do a complete training and explain all aspects of a process, the different tasks get separated and included in small five minutes online-trainings. As the trainings are short, employees stay motivated and concentrated. A series of micro-learnings replaces the traditional longer web-trainings.[60] If required, single episodes can get fostered and repeated individually. At the end human and machine learning is quite similar.

---

[60] Henz, Patrick (2017): "Access Granted – Tomorrow's Business Ethics"

A2-14 THE HEART OF A.I.

Artificial Intelligence is a software and due to this acts on algorithm and pre-defined orders. Software and robots which can re-program itself are still science fiction, even though scientists are already experimenting with such solutions. Due to this, the character of the AI depends heavily on the programmer team, the "creators".

Based on this relation, this group is sensible for the company. It not only requires the highest talents, but furthermore an effective team play. The team has to represent the complete company, including all its values and diversity.

Different languages are a key factor for diversity. This as thinking influences language and language influences thinking. The philosophical question what was first, thought or word, is still not solved. What studies confirm is that multinational teams are more efficient than single national groups. Different languages not only consists of different vocabulary, but furthermore different grammar and structures. People coming from different culture perceive their environment differently. If such employees can work efficiently together, if confronted with a problem, the group will come up with more ideas how to solve this.

The benefits of language goes further, "speaking an additional language provides greater cognitive and emotional understanding than just the native tongue."[61] With this, the programmer group has an easier access to understand the requirements of the company and elaborate empathy not only for their needs, but also for other stakeholders, who will be directly or non-directly with the AI. High levels of diversity ensures that the code of the AI will not include cultural or other bias.

---

[61] Hogan-Brun, Gabrielle (2017): "People who speak multiple languages make the best employees for one big reason"

Patrick Henz

A2-15 DATA PRIVACY FOR THE DIGITAL TWIN

Digitalization plays an important part inside Industry 4.0. Production and test facilities, but also office infrastructure can be simulated inside the computer. This virtual structures can run in parallel to the real-world locations and as the "Digital Twin" receives continuous information from its counterpart, the simulation gets more adequate.

The Digital Twin is used to analyze the efficiency of the complex system, especially to predict how it reacts to changes. An important tool to understand when are which updates requires, or for example, when temporary downtimes have to be planned to install required spare parts.

The idea is not completely new, as Sid Meier's 1990 Railroad Tycoon is only one example for successful economic simulations, played on MS-DOS and the then actual Amiga- and Atari-home computers.

If we follow Edward Deming's philosophy, employees are part of the system. So not only the change of hard- and software will determine the output, but also the change of employees between the different positions. This based on skills and experience. If we think of other games, as sports management simulations, companies may not only include long-term skills into the digital twin, but also the actual performance of the employee, including medical leaves and the last results from the regular evaluations. Similar to soccer players or other athletes, corporate employees not constantly work on their highest levels, but are influenced by mood, distraction, health and other factors.

The computer simulation is not limited to picture the machine or structures, but also could save digital twins of its employees. These characters can include all available HR information, so that an AI can analyze on which position the employee is most effective and furthermore predict potential the performance.

But not only the HR department is a potential source of information, it can come also from automated devices. Today's voice-based interfaces are integrated into smart phones and operation systems. They achieved a higher independence thanks to intelligent loudspeakers, as Amazon's Alexa. Here the AI is not an additional app, but the device was designed around this software. The AI is connected to the Cloud, so that all requests get analyzed and even stored as big data. An industrial solution would send such data to the company server, where it may get connected to the HR-files or included into the Digital Twin. These interfaces could be connected to most machinery and thanks to this, Industry 4.0 solutions adapt to the user and not the other way around. Nevertheless, adequate skills are required. As the interface is not only connecting human with the machine, but furthermore is online with the server, it is capable to analyze the user commands, including its results. The human is completely transparent and the company is always aware on what level of efficiency he or she performs.

To deliver the most accurate results, the simulation has to include the employee's long-term skills, but also the changing short-term conditions. As companies may give access to their external partners to use the digital twin, it is understandable that data privacy regulations are imperative. This to protect the individual's fundamental right of privacy and in addition to this, to protect the company against the possibility that an external partner would woos away talent. Digital Twins may be driven by the company's IT- or project management department. Normally, they are not specialized on data privacy or human labor-law. For this it is required that HR and Compliance accept the changing environment with its new roles and responsibilities. To limit legal risks, these departments have to be included in the design, setup and execution of the Digital Twin, especially as different countries or regions, as the European Union are implementing more restrictive data privacy laws. Mostly such regulations do not prohibit the usage of personal data, but requires from the organization to be transparent with the data it collects and which algorithm predict for what purpose.

Digital Twins are not limited on technical processes, but also can get used to picture white collar processes. Products like Microsoft's Office 365[62] are able to understand, based on emails and calendar data, communication patterns and give insights who in the office work frequently together. Based on such information, offices can get re-designed to facilitate communication, as grouping employees together and so bring communication from on- to off-line. In most companies are employees allowed to use office IT infrastructure also privately, so depending on local, such additional insights may cause data privacy concerns[63], especially at it may include also externals.

---

[62] Microsoft (fetched 08.11.2017): Microsoft Workplace Analytics

[63] Tushman, Michael L. / Kahn, Anna / Porray, Mary Elizabeth / Binns, Andy (2017): "Email and Calendar Data Are Helping Firms Understand How Employees Work"

A2-16 ENZO 4.0 – The Digital Counselor

Actual technologies make it possible to create an electronic version of a human actor. This not only gets used to create alien characters, but also to bring back passed away actors to the silver-screen. Of course, this is always connected with discussions about ethics, as the dead cannot read the script or deny a role. Less problematic is to create a younger version of the actor, if the story requires such. The last was done, for example, for the movie "Terminator Genisys", as a younger version of Arnold Schwarzenegger's character was in need.

What about simulating not only the individual's outer appearance and movements, but his or her mind? Empathic and knowledgeable advisors are important for employees to take the right decision, but it is not always possible to have such around.

Artificial Intelligence can make this possible. Based on information like biographies and documentations, software designers can create a chat-bot with the required character and knowledge, including its strengths and weaknesses. This is the starting point, as the software will learn thru the continuous interactions with its human students. Based on the programmed character, the chat-bot perceives information and processes it. In this process the software connects today's topics with the simulated attitudes and believes. As result, leaders from the past can give relevant advise for today's challenges. The sophisticated software is based on a cloud-server and with apps connects to the user. With this, the counselor is independent from locations, as thanks to smart phones and watches, the user can activate it. Furthermore, the AI is capable of multitasking and attends several users at the same time.

New inventions come with new legal challenges. The AI learns through additional information and the conversations with the users. If the software does not keep the different user accounts separated, it can learn much faster, as it learns from a big number of users instead of just one. On the other hand, experiments showed that humans build up a relation of trust with a robot or even other kind of machine. Due to this, they may discuss confidential information with the AI. If the user accounts are not strictly separated, the software uses the confidential information to learn, and counsel other users. Even if it not directly forwards the information, it will become the base of guidance.

Companies can take this idea and create such an app for internal use, where they recreate their founders. An interesting idea, as for many of these figures starting their own company was not only a way to earn money, but they had a vision that their products and solutions could change the market or even whole societies. As conclusion, they had been aware that taking on short-term risks could jeopardize the future of the company, sustainability had a high importance for them. The interaction with the founder's digital twin may create a disruptive moment, what is required that the employee can re-think his or her decision; this to avoid getting rushed to into a wrong agreement.

The technology can go further. Already today exist applications which analyze the user's behavior to conclude on his or her mood, including state of mind. This up to understand when the human individual is in a depressive state and may think about suicide. The app is not passive to answer the user's questions, but gets effective when a special behavior triggers it. The reaction can be the start of a discussion, but also that the software automatically contacts the organization's Human Resources-department. Again, a relevant usage, but requires robust data privacy processes.

First Virtual Counselors may come from a non-expected side. The video game industry licenses sports leagues and events directly from the official organizers. This way they are able to simulate the original teams including the real players. The actual "FIFA Soccer" titles not only feature the outer appearance of the original stars, but also their individual strengths and weaknesses. Such a digital twin can include also values as honesty, as the simulation may include a tendency to foul or not. Less obviously, the video game not only simulates the soccer players, but also the coaches, as every team plays with different strategies.

We already have the technical possibility to simulate real humans, as it is possible instead of creating the individual style of playing, picture the individual's philosophy of life and business. We can imagine that in a near future a Playstation game as "Ferrari Racing Legends" not only includes detailed digital twins of the original race cars from up to 70 years ago, but also Enzo Ferrari himself, who not only interacts with us, but learns from these dialogues.

The impression gets more impressive, if not only the outer appearance is near to the original, but also the voice. Startups, but also established companies, are working on AI algorithms, which can analyze speech samples and offers an application the possibility to speak with the same tone.[64] This gives the user the ability to include additional words into the recorded voice or create complete new speeches. Similar to today, where we can manipulate reality on photos and video, it will be tomorrow also possible to do this with voice recordings.[65] This opens up ethical concerns, as it will become easier to create "fake news", but also as human individuals may tend to humanize computer applications.

[64] Vincent, James (2017): "Lyrebird claims it can recreate any voice using just one minute of sample audio"

[65] Statt, Nick (2016): "Adobe is working on an audio app that lets you add words someone never said"

That way the digital counselor is similar to a digital twin, only that the AI is not created based on an existing individual, but an idealized, and so partly fictive, character. Also the purpose is different, the classic digital twin wants to simulate reality and the AI counselor to influence and advice human individuals.

In many ways Industry 4.0 lowers the economics of scale and with this the advantage of big organizations. Additional to this, Artificial Intelligence is in the process to replace human workers, including white collar employees. The more standardized the position, the higher the risk to get replaced. The best protection for the human is to have a creative job-position. As even though AIs will be capable to create art, human customers appreciate the human expression. Doing business may get similar to the first half of 20th Century again, where car manufacturers developed the vehicle it-selves, but external coach companies designed and build the car's body individually to the specific needs and the customer's wishes. That way some of Ferrari's most famous and beautiful cars arose. It is no surprise that Enzo himself not liked industrial mass production, but understood himself and the company as creative craftsmen. Based on his decisions, the workshop's employees crafted the individual cars. Art on the highest quality level.[66]

Intelligent software can take on administrative tasks and combined with 3D-printing, employees can create individual pieces for relative low costs. Thanks to this, a more individual car production gets possible again. Similar to today's craft beer market, smaller automobile manufacturers get the opportunity to compete against big organizations. Or at least work together with them to take the mass product and include individual changes, like a different body. This is an opportunity, but no automatic development, as artists are rare. If such a talent is not available, the solutions from the craftsmen would not be more creative as the industrial mass product.

The possibilities of the new technology open up great opportunities. Some of them existed before and will come back. A discussion with Enzo Ferrari's Digital Twin would be a great support to understand its opportunities and challenges from a complete different angle. Disruption!

---

[66] Henz, Patrick (2017): "Business Philosophy according to Enzo Ferrari"

A2-17 THE STRANGEST THINGS

Netflix's hit series "The Stranger Things" sends us back into the eighties. A time where video-games still had been at maximum two-dimensional. Space Invader's laser cannon could go to the left and right, it moved on just one dimension X. Pac Man ran through a labyrinth, he used already two dimensions, X and Y. In opposite to these electronic games had been roleplay adventures a la Dungeons & Dragons en vogue. Even if existed miniature figures, the game visualized inside the player's imagination, as a game master read from a book and explained the challenges, a real 3D-experience. In addition to the group games, there had been also published several solo adventures as books. The reader had the possibility to decide in different situations how the character should react. Depending this, he or she continues reading on a different page. Based on the combination of decisions, it was always a different story to experience.

Time is generally defined as the fourth dimension. If we define that it is possible to move free inside the dimensions, it would be possible to move in time from beginning to end, and end to beginning. Similar to rewind a VHS-tape. A general possibility, but based on the limitation of our existence not possible for a human. Just as Pac Man is not able to escape his two-dimensional labyrinth. The consequence of a four dimensional universe would be that the free will is an illusion, as everything already is decided. Due to this, humans would not be accountable for their actions and decisions.

If we analyze our life, sometimes small decisions had a big impact. If we had acted differently back in time, our today's life would be completely different. Actual theories indicate that there may exist a nearly infinity number of dimensions, so practically each decision would open up a new universe.[67] The Big Bang was not only the start of a three dimensional spreading over the time, but furthermore the unfolding of universes. Concluding this theory, there exists for each action a consequence and each possible decision had been taken in a different dimension. Ergo, the individual is free to choose and can be hold responsible. This philosophy underlines the rule of law, as the human is responsible for its actions, no excuse. As everything what can be imagined, happened in some far-away universe, we have to take care that Pac Man does not stand behind us.[68]

---

[67] Howell, Elizabeth (2016): "Parallel Universes: Theories & Evidence"

[68] Henz, Patrick (2017): "Access Granted – Tomorrow's Business Ethics"

Patrick Henz

A2-18 ARTISTS NEEDED

Today's technology offers numerous possibilities to disrupt today's business or life in general. Still lacking is often creativity to identify a real benefit. Virtual Reality glasses are on the market. Thanks to the Google Cardboard[69], such glasses can be acquired for very accessible prices, what makes them interesting also for schools and students. Especially for learning purpose, 3D videos are interesting, even without direct interaction. The learning effect raises with involvement. The virtual reality mediathek by the German public television broadcaster ZDF presents such an example, as one of their videos teleports the user inside the historic Roman Colosseum.[70] Important that there is no single position, but thanks to the glasses, the individual stands sometimes between the fighting gladiators and later besides the imperator. To follow the action it is required to change the viewing angle to look in different directions. Due to this, the user cannot sit in chair, but has to stand up, just as inside the virtual experience. If this is not the case, it is impossible to follow the plot.

The story gets not automatically presented, but has to be discovered. Due to human psychology, what is more difficult to receive, perceives a higher valorization. Information, which had been concluded by the individual itself, gets easier remembered than such, which had been directly presented. So, if used with creativity, VR glasses does not only can offer a more plastic experience, but also support the learning effect. Only one more problem, many individuals feel nausea while using these devices. This problem arises because of the disconnect between eyes and the inner ears, where the human sense of equilibrium is located. While using the glasses, eyes and ears receive different information, what the human body interprets this as nausea. So far a relevant problem, which prevents the further commercial success of the VR glasses. So no surprise that different companies work on

---

[69] Google Cardboard (fetched 28.08.2017)

[70] ZDF (2017): "Gladiatoren im Kollosseum"

the problem.[71]

Even if no learning effect is required, the artist can bring the technological possibilities to a higher level. This is comparable to painters as Pablo Picasso, who used the screen not to picture reality, but to create art. Based on this philosophy, Commodore Inc. invited pop art artist Andy Warhol to present in 1985 their new Amiga computer. In opposite to other machines, this 16-bit computer had the ability to show up to 4096 colors on the screen. As the Amiga was completely new, the engineers had not been completely sure if the software would run stable on the new machine. Luckily the presentation went well, and Warhol edited live a photo of the also invited Blondie singer Debbie Harrie. An impressive start for the Amiga, which should sell later more than six million units.

Today, creativity can be often found in the independent gaming scene. The big commercial studios invest millions of dollars to create new titles. Similar to the movie industry, this often blocks creativity, as the financial success is mandatory to ensure sustainability of the business. Questions if to realize a new concept or to publish the successor of an already established successful game mostly gets decided for the last. Similar to classic arcade titles independent programmers can create art, without 3D graphics or professional soundtracks, but mainly based on an unique idea.

Smart phones apps offer additional possibilities, as the specific location can get included, even the direction, in which the user looks. New possibilities for the artists to infuse interactivity to the videos, as used by the Foo Fighters. Their app combined a performance of "Sky is a Neighborhood" with a view on the user's starry sky.[72] Underlying the song's message, the app gave the user additional information to the constellations. This knowledge supported the feeling of a cosmic neighborhood.

With this, put on your VR glasses to experience, "A Day in the Future"…

---

[71] Metz, Rachel (2017): "Now There's a Nausea Dial for Virtual Reality"

[72] sky.foofighters.com (2017): "Sky is a Neighborhood"

A2-19 A DAY IN THE FUTURE

She still could remember that ten years ago, when she started her profession as Compliance Officer, integrity was about humans and defined as "value-based behavior". The business environment back then was as complicated as today, so it had been an important concept, as personal integrity helped the employees to guide in situations, which not had been defined anymore by laws and guidelines.

Integrity means that values and behavior are in a correct positive relation. As humans are complex creatures, this relations is less obvious than it sounds.

- We have two given variables: "values" and "behavior". Normally the behavior should be motivated and based on one's own values. But this does not automatically has to be the case. The strength of the values (and derived attitudes) determinates how easily behavior can be distracted from the values, for example through temptations or urgent needs. Values and attitudes are learnt in the different stages of socialization.
- If we have such a situation that values and behavior are not compatible anymore, the individual feels being outside its normal state of harmony. Based on Leon Festinger's "theory of cognitive dissonance"[73], the person perceives now an inner pressure to get back into harmony again.[74] For this, he or she can adapt the two variables "values" (= "cognition") and "behavior". Of course, normally the values should be stronger and so resistant to a change, but if the person took a non-value based decision several times or in an important decision, the individual is not sure anymore if this is really a value and furthermore decides from the observed own behavior that there must be a complete different value behind, from which this action is related from. With this logical process,

---

[73] Festinger, Leon (1957): „A Theory of Cognitive Dissonance"

[74] Fischer, Lorenz / Wiswede, Guenter (1997): „Grundlagen der Sozialpsychologie"

the human being is with the new assumed value in harmony again, as this new one is compatible with the own behavior.

She liked philosophy and had been familiar with Ayn Rand's work, especially her main piece "Atlas Shrugged". Here Rand wrote: *"Achievement of your happiness is the only moral purpose of your life, and that happiness, not pain or mindless self-indulgence, is the proof of your moral integrity, since it is the proof and the result of your loyalty to the achievement of your values."*

As responsible Compliance Officer, she wanted to support the employees to find their happiness at the work-place. To achieve that she explained the company's values and why they are not only relevant for the organization, but also for the employees and society. For other training events she used different cases to discuss ethical blindness, especially to make people aware how difficult and stressful situations could manipulate their behavior. Emotions. Strong positive and negative emotions could non-adequately influence decisions, until individuals act against their own personal values and attitudes.

It was a rainy afternoon and she went for another cup of coffee to continue analyzing the algorithm of the Artificial Intelligence's software. Today, her tasks became more complicated. Intelligent software replaced around 40% of the human workforce, including positions, where it became responsible to take relevant decisions for the organization. Nevertheless, everything still is based on human integrity, as even the more advanced software still operates based on the coding done by human software designers. For this, the programmers became one of her focus groups. Ironically, they had been hired with the support of the HR AI software to ensure that the new employees are a perfect fit for the organization and represent an adequate diversity. The last was key, as diverse groups seem to produce the best results and different point of views not only infuse fresh ideas, but make the group also less vulnerable against psychological pressures, known as "ethical blindness".

Even with positive values and the best coding, the AI's decision could only be as good as the used information to come to it. For this, one of her daily routines in the morning was to ensure that the required information streams are reaching the AI. On the screen she could see the number of messages, including their size in megabyte. Even if a filter tried to identify "fake news", she daily ensured the efficiency of the software with taking samples from the out-filtered group, but also the ones which passed the test. At the end, artificial and human employees are not that different, if they work with flawed information, their decisions and output will be negative. The integrity of data was a priority. A risk, as hackers not had been limited to enter directly the company's IT infrastructure, but could sabotage the flow of information, even before it arrived at the company.

Besides the regular monitoring, from time to time she analyzed the AI's algorithm directly. This to have a control that no one added some lines, which not belonged inside the software and would alter its behavior. Her big challenge was the autonomous learning-part. The AI analyzed the incoming information and learnt from it. Based on this, the software adapted its decisions. All this data had been stored on a server, but she was not able to read it as the software's original code. The only possibility was to perform different stress tests with the AI. She created several business scenarios, some pretty usual, some rare. Luckily the software not showed any problems so far. The only concern had been the way the AI communicated with other AIs. In the beginning the machines used standard English, but after a short while started to develop their own language, which seemed more efficient for them. Good for the software, bad for her, as for humans it was not understandable at all.

Besides that she felt optimistic that also the coming audit by the country's Department of Artificial Intelligence would go smoothly.

Nearly time to go home. Before she shut off her computer, she still checked a last time her favorite news portals. In this moment she realized that there was no clear separation between artificial and human employees anymore, but instead a grey area. Even if she not had any microchips implemented, as some of her co-workers, she depended on the internet and could not imagine a life without. Her smart phone apps practically became a part of her.

With the last sip of coffee she closed the door of her office to drive home.

A2-20 ARTIFICIAL INTELLIGENCE ACCORDING TO PHILIP K. DICK: WHY ANDROIDS DREAM

US author Philip K. Dick wrote around 40 novels and 120 short-stories on his writing machine. With this classic tool he created claustrophobic science fiction scenarios, writing less about alien invasions, but artificial intelligence. Doing so, he not only described technical possibilities, but furthermore described ethical concerns. Most of his stories featured different layers of reality, what his work compares to Franz Kafka. As all good science fiction, his stories were less an escape from reality, but the opposite, allowed us a view into a distorted mirror.

Ridley Scott took the book "Do Androids Dream of Electric Sheep?" and converted it into arthouse science fiction movie. His masterpiece starts with a scene where a Blade Runner is conducts the Voight-Kampff-Test to define if the individual on the other side of the table is human or artificial. This as it was forbidden for the so-called replicants to return to Earth.[75] The idea of the test was to trigger small deviations in the android's behavior, which would reveal its artificial origin. With this, the Voight-Kampff-method was similar to the Turing-test, a process developed in 1950 by the British mathematician and computer scientist Alan Turing.[76] His idea was to confirm artificial intelligence by its ability to pretend being a human. For the test purpose a panel of experts communicated text-only with humans and different software. If the software could achieve that the majority of participants assume to write with a human instead with a software, the AI passed the test.

The movie is based on Philip K. Dick's book *"Do Androids Dream of Electric Sheep?"*[77] The author developed the interesting concept that machines received human memories to ground them. Related to today's knowledge

---

[75] Scott, Ridley (1982): "Blade Runner"

[76] The Alan Turing Internet Scrapbook (2014): "The Turing Test, 1950"

[77] Dick, Philip K. (1968): "Do Androids Dream of Electric Sheep?"

about Artificial Intelligence, this idea makes sense. Based on its code, the software is capable of autonomous learning and adapting its behavior to that. With doing so, today's software is not re-programming its own code, but storing the learned information. If a new situation gets identified to be similar to one in the past, the software will execute a script of a learned behavior. The more successful the result had been and the more similar the new situation perceived to the earlier one, the higher the possibility that the known behavior gets repeated. Furthermore, the AI can analyze different behavior scripts to identify patterns and underlined values & attitudes. If such are identified, the software can elaborate adequate behaviors also for unknown scenarios.

The AI's codes defines limited behavior and enables the machine to learn. Quite similar to a child. At this point the software is not effective yet to use for its planned purpose. The AI can start with its tasks, but the error-rate is still high. With new gained experience the quality of decision making raises. To ensure transparency in the coding and flexibility to adapt to new situations, the software designers do not want to program behavior scripts into the original codes, but let the machine learn for itself. As companies do it with their human talents, a coach may support the newly installed AI to learn faster. This individual accompanies the AI and analyzes together with it the quality of taken decisions.

Instead of investing time on machine learning, copying experiences from one AI to another may speed up the process. Here the manufacturer of the AI (our *"Tyrell Corporation"*) lets the prototype act and learn in a simulated environment, which is a near as possible to the later real environment. The advantage of having the training outside the client's location is to avoid active and / or passive sabotage by unengaged employees. Most probably the AI will not be added to existing human workforce, but on the long-run replace a certain numbers of individuals, so they may not like to support the machine. Such sabotage could be a physical damage to the computer or a simple slow and non-productive working, so that the AI could not effectively learn from its future colleagues.

When done at the manufacturer's test location, the results of these deep-learning will be copied later to the memories of the sold AIs. This process supports adequate behaviors, as the software does not have to start with 0 and use pure trial-and-error. The AI perceives the experiences as its own and identify it as successful behavior of the past. Behavior scripts used various times in the past are relatively protected against an easy change. This as adequate behavior not guaranties the wished results, but always includes a risk factor. If the script has a 95% possibility to lead to the favorable outcome, the AI will continue using it, even if in 5% there will be a failure. Mathematically, if the machine already executed 10,000 process, a negative result will not lead to a change of behavior. Here it does not matter, if the AI really executed these 10,000 processes or only perceives that it did so.

Of course the AI saves such experiences in a much more abstract way than Dick described it in its novel, but nevertheless the concepts are comparable. The advantage of using "fake memories" instead of including the desired behavior directly in the AI's algorithm is that the software stays relatively small and non-complicated. With this it is efficient and can adapt fast to new situations. Simplicity ensures the basic principles of machine learning: fairness, accountability and transparency.[78] Dick not only used this idea for "Do Androids dream of Electric Sheep?", but also addressed this topic in another novel: "Total Recall"[79]. As human and artificial behavior are similar, once the faked memories had been implanted into androids, once into humans. As Hosagrahar Visvesvaraya Jagadish from the University of Michigan pointed out, most suboptimal AI (or also human) decisions are not caused by biased code, but can be explained by the usage of non-correct information. This as sources mostly not gets chosen by the AI itself, but a human individual.

Today's smart phones are continuously connected to the internet, this to ensure that the user receives actual push messages. We can conclude that androids would work accordingly, at least if they stay inside the range of a mobile network. Nevertheless even in future such replicants could not stay

---

[78] www.fatml.org (2017): "Fairness, Accountability, and Transparency in Machine Learning"

[79] Dick, Philip K. (1966) "Total Recall"

inside such a radius all of the time. In the movie they escaped from the colonies to return to Earth, so they had not been able to connect to a Cloud. For this, they require the ability to act independent from such a connection.

Ethereum[80] was originally developed in 2015. The philosophy was to establish a robust peer-to-peer network to exchange information or even group resources to execute sophisticated apps. Thanks to this, central servers are not required. Androids can use a similar technology. If the connection to the central server is not available, the machines can connect with the nearest android, which can be connected to another or directly with the Cloud. Oral languages are not required for the connection between different AIs, Bluetooth-like technology enables them to communicate via "telepathy".

As today's electric cars show, batteries require time for charging. Even if scientists experiment with electric highways, we can assume that also in future it will not possible to recharge batteries everywhere. As conclusion, androids require time-off, similar to human sleep. Philip K. Dick asked if they dream of electric sheep. Dreaming machines sound illogical, but if we use again smart phones as comparison, we see that night times often get used for mayor updates on apps and even the operation system itself. This, as such processes may require an hour or even longer.

Androids may use their charging time to update their software, up to interchange information with the Cloud and other androids. Similar to synchronizing an iPhone with its iTunes, this makes perfect sense. The received information, as others' experiences, can be understood as dreams. In opposite to humans, AIs are available to remember their complete dream sequences and add them to their memory. Explained by a cognitive anchor-effect[81], the information can be used as base for future decisions. The more graphic the dream, the more effective the learning effect. It is no surprise that companies seek to hire the best dream designers (as seen in Blade Runner 2049) and due to this, dream sequences would be protected by

---

[80] Ethereum (2017): "Blockchain App Platform"

[81] Tversky, Amos / Kahnemann, Daniel (1974): "Judgment under Uncertainty: Heuristics and Biases"

copyright law. For the case that there is no connection to the Cloud or other sleeping machines, it will be a dreamless sleep.

Philip K. Dick hinted it his book, But Ridley Scott's movie Blade Runner had been more direct, as the name *"android"* had been changed to *"replicant"*, a wording with an open negative touch. In 2014 the *"hitchBOT"* hiked across Canada. To do so, scientists sat the little robot on the side of an highway with a message that it wants to travel and meet new friends. Then they tracked how drivers reacted to the machine. If they helped hitchBOT, ignored or even destroyed it. Even if there had been single bad experiences, the overall results had been quite promising.[82] Of course, its likeable design made it easy to like the little machine. Today scientists evaluate the results of the experiment and these may confirm that that humans are possible to build up an emotional relation with a machine. Such may positive or negative. A relevant conclusion, as the implementation of AI in an organization is a disruptive situation, which pushes the individuals out of their comfort zone. If no adequate change management is in place, emotional reactions as sabotage is a risk. The concept for many AIs and robots is to work and act together with their human employees, is underlined with the expression "cobot"[83]. Just as in "Blade Runner 2049", where the replicant "K" works in the police department together with his human colleagues,[84] often suffering from their rejection. It is important to overcome this state of distrust.

To process his personal defeat against IBM's "Deep Blue", Chess Grand Master Garry Kasparov organized a "freestyle chess tournament" where groups of humans, chess programs and mixed human-AI-teams could join and play against each other. To his surprise, a team of average players, using average chess programs, won the tournament, this based on a superior process. He concluded: *'Weak human + machine + better process was superior to a strong computer alone and, more remarkably, superior to a strong human + machine + inferior process.'*[85]

---

[82] Hitchbot (fetched 10.6.2016)

[83] Silverman, Rachel Emma (2000): "The Words of Tomorrow"

[84] Villeneuve, Denis (2017): "Blade Runner 2049"
[85] Kasparov, Garry (2010): "The Chess Master and the Computer"

Furthermore, in a negative atmosphere it gets overseen that AI can act as ambassador for humanity, as non-governmental organizations. For example, a bot can act as a first basic legal or medical support for groups, which up to day had no access to such support. The *"donotpay"*-project created such a robot lawyer.[86] Today the software can support for free if people seek for compensation for delayed planes, help against unfair parking or speeding tickets. So far, the target group could be everybody inside the society. But thanks to relative cheap devices as basic smart phones or tablets, also more vulnerable groups could get support, for example related immigration questions or also healthcare checks.[87] As Tyrell's claim promised: *"More human than human."*

---

[86] Do not Pay (fetched 20.03.2017)

[87] Brown, Jessica (2017): "The robot lawyer that helped people with their parking tickets is now helping refugees"

A2-21 ZOMBIFICATION

The human spirit faces limitations by the body. To ensure adequate behavior, we have to be aware of these.

Jet lag and missing sleep can lead to limitations of cognitive capabilities, as for example, awareness, decision making and argumentation.[88] Due this, employees, who travel over different time-zones are vulnerable for safety- and corruption-risks. A twelve hour flight, especially when it was in tourist-class, temporary sends the individual back from a higher level in Maslow's Pyramid right to the bottom. Arriving at the airport immigration we often have the only wish to reach the hotel. With this we are an easy victim for a governmental official, who asks us for a bribe or facilitation payment. Being on the first level means that we only care about the actual survival, long-term planning only start of the second level. We do not have the energy to argue, but might decide to give the money to leave this place as fast as possible. Zombie-like we seem not to have a free will anymore. This status will change after some hours of good sleep.

Additionally to this, language skills get lost, if not used regularly. So employees may need some days until they are back into the different language. Such negative jet lag effects are not completely to avoid, but an adequate preparation and healthy lifestyle help. So the health initiatives of numerous companies not only support to reduce the sickness-level, but furthermore are a protection against accidents and potential corruption-cases. Especially facilitation payments and low value corruption work with the idea to make the individual tired of resisting. Mainly with non-transparent and bureaucratic arguments. To resist this, the employee needs self-confidence and will-power to stand up.[89]

---

[88] Martin, Jennifer L. (fetched 29.4.2017): "Travel & Jet Lag"

[89] Henz, Patrick (2017): "Wirtschaftspsychologie und Compliance"

Another risk factor is disinterest. For the Ethics & Compliance Officer it is not enough to inform about laws and guidelines, but he or she has to motivate the employees. This is imperative as it is impossible to control individuals all the time, especially when they are in remote locations. Employees get motivated if they understand the company's strategy and how their individual contribution supports the long-term sustainability of the organization. Furthermore, information can raise empathy for the victims and cost of corruption.

Bored employees are a risk factor, as defense is down and potential red flags do not get identified. Such individuals are more likely to be involved in an accident and are an easy victim for cognitive hackers or even corrupt governments officials. Fun, or at least interest in the daily work should be given. Of course we cannot all work inside a funky new economy lounge office, but nevertheless, employers can motivate their workforce by treating them as humans and not machines. If employees understand how their individual input leads to the success of the organization, they are not only motivated, but also less vulnerable against psychological biases. The Compliance department can directly support this, not only thru its own workshops, but also to review tools and processes, to ensure that they not foster a "check-the-box"-mentality instead to give the individual responsibility to think for his- or her-self. Of course, Compliance hast to be near in business to be the required partner for questions and discussions. This does also not mean that Compliance has to give up all processes and controls, but they have to be adequate to manage the given risks. Anything less opens up a risk, everything more also.

A2-22 „I AM A RACER"

Formula One driver Michael Schumacher said once: *"I am a racer, I push things to the absolute edge."* His career is the best proof of the statement. After winning twice the championship with Benetton in 1994 and '95, he left his personal comfort zone to join the Scuderia Ferrari. At that time he could have stayed with Benetton and had been the favorite to win the title also in '96. Nevertheless he did this, as for most racers, his goal was not only to win the championship, but to win it with the most prestigious team.[90] Doing so, he had been well aware that this change would not only include driving, but he would have the addional challenge to build up the whole team to achieve competiveness. This goal was, of course, not to reach in the next season, but took Schumacher five years. But then it became an impressive series as he won the championship from 2000 to '04. After the '06-season he retired as an active driver to become an advisor for Ferrari.

2000: Ferrari F1 2000, 3.0L, V12, 770hp, 600kg.

As a born racer, he needed the competition, even if it was not about to win titles, but just go to his personal limits. He not only practiced sky diving, but started in 2008 an '09 also in the IDM Superbike-series. An accident here prevented a temporary Formula One-comeback to replace Felipe

---

[90] Henz, Patrick (2017): "Business Philosophy according to Enzo Ferrari"

Massa.

Besides being a racer, Schumacher always uses his privileged position to give back and support numerous charity organizations.[91] Even if he had sports-spirit and a sense of justice, in the heat of the moment he lost these in some race situations. After an accident with his direct competitor Jacques Villeneuve at the final race of the '97 tournament, he got disqualified, not only for the race, but the complete drivers' championship.

Nothing special related to him, in fact similar black-outs happened to Ayrton Senna, Luis Hamilton or Sebastian Vettel. All good sportsmen which are supporting charity, all of them "success seekers". These characters tend to overestimate their own abilities and underestimate the risks of the situation. For the "failure avoiders" it is the other way around. Thanks to self-selection the first group of people will try to get more risky tasks with the goal that they can prove their selves and advance faster in their career, they will apply to positions in sales or become a race driver. In sudden and new projects they see the opportunity, but not the risk.[92] Based on this characteristics, they are vulnerable for psychological pressures, known as "ethical blindness". As Schumacher pointed out, racers act on the limit. The red line to not only be at limit, but in fact, to overstep it is quite thin. In fact we have a risk group in a risky environment: a double risk.

The Human Resources department sooner or later will implement Artificial Intelligence software. This to support the hiring process, but also continuously to manage the employees' individual careers. AI is, first of all, not about collecting data, but to analyze and apply it to elaborate effective predictions. The first generation of such software is already available and different organizations implemented it. Due to this, the AI can understand, for example with analyzing the CVs or being used in job interviews, what is the individual's character, if they are success seekers or failure avoiders. In addition to this, the next generation of HR software will be able to predict how individuals would react in different situations, including stressful scenarios. Such predictions may influence promotions and the development

---

[91] www.michael-schumacher.de (fetched 11.08.2017): "Giving Back"

[92] Henz, Patrick (2017): "Business Philosophy according to Enzo Ferrari"

of individual careers in general. Similar to the *"Minority Report"*[93], employees may get limited, before they did anything wrong. Of course, this opens up ethical issues. If an organization decides to use this software, it has to be transparent for the employee, including that he or she receives access to the results. If such present risk factors, the person be given the opportunity to work on the factors. Similar to the analyzing of hand-writing, local governments may forbid the usage of such AI predictions.

For the Ethics & Compliance department detailed predictions are not necessary, a general insight, if the employees are "success seekers" and "failure avoiders" is relevant to understand how the communication and workshop to the different target groups has to be. The HR AI may give further insight, but it is not clear, how much progress this offers. Thanks to self-selection, the two groups apply for positions, which fit to their individual characters. Based on experience, the Compliance personnel should be able to identify the two groups even with intelligent software.

There are two key messages for racers:

- The "three-minute-rule": There is no urgency in business that there is not time for a cup of coffee / tea. Even short breaks can prevent that an employee gets rushed into a decision, when in reality he or she is not ready to make such. If possible a person should sleep at least one night before making an important choice. If possible, discussions of the topic with a colleague, friend or family member can further support to get a different point of view.

- "Choose your battles": An important message for the success seeker, who feels the inner need to always compete. This as the decision-making is tiring and as conclusion individuals have only a limited amount of mental energy available.[94] If you waste your limited resources on non-necessary decision making processes, you

---

[93] Dick, Philip K. (1956): "The Minority Report"

[94] Weller, Chris (2017): "A neuroscientist who studies decision-making reveals the most important choice you can make."

may not have these available later, if they are needed for important suddenly upcoming topics. As result, the quality of decision making is suffering and may lead to non-adequate choices, up to violation of law, social norm and guidelines.

For racers the first point is difficult to follow, as in opposite to business reality, speed and reflexes are priority. There is not possibility to make a pit-stop before a relevant overtaking maneuver. The second idea is included in the continuous development of the race car. If not prohibited by regulations, engineers try to make the driving as easy as possible for the drivers. Computer programs analyze the car's setup and sensors control the tires. With this, the drivers need less concentration on the tires' conditions, as the computer knows when it is best to come in for a change. A highly relevant update was the implementation of automated shifting. Now the driver could forget the hundreds of shifts inside a race. A big workload was taken off the drivers' shoulders. This highly appreciated as racers, like Michael Schumacher, could shift up and down by pressing buttons on the steering wheel, instead to take off the hand from the wheel, shift, put hand back on the wheel, and so on.

With this we are back to Artificial Intelligence, as based on smart data (statistically and reasonable connected big data) the software can calculate the results of different choices. Not only the direct own ones, but furthermore the later decisions of competitors and other stake holders. Such complex simulations support the employee, meaning the employee requires less usage of the limited mental energy.

With or without AI, the Ethics&Compliance Officer has to be close to the business. This is not limited to the implementation of local Compliance Champions, but also means to understand the business. If this is given, an employee does not have to invest much mental energy for the contact. An adequate tone from the top is required so that even racers understand that sometimes it is necessary to skip a race to win the championship. If the employee is missing the required information, it is a sign of strength to ask and avoid non-necessary assumption. As Stephen Hawking said: *"The greatest enemy of knowledge is not ignorance, it is the illusion of knowledge."*

Patrick Henz

A2-23 GAMIFICATION^2

Gamification is mostly seen as a possibility to communicate information. But the development went already one step further. The prestigious University of Geneva will partner up with the science-fiction online game EVE. The university will provide 167,000 deep space light curve images to the game community, where the users can use their virtual space ships to explore this information and support science to discover new exoplanets. EVE Online includes up 500,000 players and due to this, presents a relevant source to support the chronically understaffed scientific projects.[95]

The game simulates a virtual world, where players can take on the role of spaceship captain and discover the wonders of the galaxy. With the connection to the university, the game becomes reality, as the users, sitting before their home computers, become scientists acting inside a virtual space. The software simulates a virtual object based on the scientific data and, inside his or her role, the human user evaluates it. If enough users evaluated the planet information, the games sends the information back to the university.

Back in 2003, EVE Online was designed as Massively Multiplayer Online Role-Playing Game (MMORPG). Today even conventional games offer an additional multiplayer option, where the users can play against others, independent where they are in the world. The Cloud makes it possible. It is up to the game-designers to explore new possibilities for this technology. But the trend that games and reality grow closer together will continue, and this not only because of the advancing graphics.

Thanks to the continuous connection to the internet, real-time information can be included into the game-play. Users could play Soccer against professional teams from the actual game day, including details as temporary excluded injured players or the actual condition of the team. Furthermore, the simulation can take the local weather conditions into the account. If it

---

[95] Fogel, Stefanie (2017): "EVE Online is crowdsourcing the search for real exoplanets"

rains outside the window, so it does inside the virtual stadium. Such additional conditions bring the game nearer to reality, as the player does not react in an independent space, but stays connected to the outside world.

The US manufacturer of wrist-worn straps that measure health information Whoop has an agreement with the NFL Players Association, which enables participating players to sell their health data to the company.[96] Worn fitness devices connected to the Cloud are an ideal possibility to include real-time information into video-games and other apps. Ethically questionable, as based on the contract, players are free to participate or not, but nevertheless the access to biometric data may be a requirement to join a top-team, so that the individual player's possibility to freely decide about his or her personal information is limited.

In opposite to "Pokemon Go" what presents "Augmented Reality" with including virtual characters into the real world, such technology would go the other way around, with including real circumstances into the virtual world, due to this it could be called "Augmented Virtuality".

Besides these possibilities, the trend may also get a dark side. Similar to the classic migrant workers of the past, "Crowd-workers" may be a similar group in the near future.[97] Artificial Intelligence will replace many white collar jobs, especially jobs with a high part of repeating tasks. These skills devalue. The replaced employees have the choice to develop new skills or offer their existing ones for a lower salary. One example for the last is that organizations will hire personnel providers for single tasks. The subcontracted employees work from home, using their private computers, connected via a virtual network to their temporary employer. Similar to today's UBER or even traditional Pizza taxis, the crowd-workers offer not only their-selves, but additionally their work-tools. What for the UBER-driver means the private car, is for the crowd-worker the private computer. This way, AI does not replace the human employee, but devalues them so far so that their usage will be cheaper than replacing them with the software. This at least until the next level of technological achievements. A

---

[96] Jones, Rhett (2017): „NFL Players Strike a Deal to Sell Their Biometric Data"

[97] Koch, Hannes (2017): "Crowdworker – die Wanderarbeiter der digitalen Generation"

potential scenario, as Stephen Hawking warned that AI and Industry 4.0 is going to reduce typical middle class jobs.[98]

UBER is already testing driverless cars and pizza delivery drones are in experimental phase. To avoid the described development of human value, different politics, but also business experts as Bill Gates and Elon Musk started a discussion to discuss a universal income, where individuals receive income from the government, independent if they work or not.

A first type of crowd-workers already exists. So far based on personal decision and part of a lifestyle. Digital nomads are individuals, which use modern telecommunication as internet and cloud to work from remote locations. With these possibilities they finance they personal interest to travel the world. As positive side effect, such temporary locations require lower costs of living than in their home countries, as mostly Europe and the US. Nomadism can further used to reduce taxes, as without having a fixed home-address, individuals may be able to construct legal tax-saving-models as open up micro companies and use offshore bank-accounts. As these modern nomads understand their business model more as lifestyle, the locations are an emotional choice. Based on cost, internet-connection, fun and safety, Berlin (Germany), Bangkok (Thailand), Budapest (Hungary), Ho Chi Minh City (Vietnam) and Chiang Mail (Thailand) are trending.[99] Digital nomads are, in most, a sub-group of the Millennials. Due to this, potential negative consequences, such an insufficient healthcare and insurances, are not measurable yet.

Unnoticed digital nomads became part of company structures. Various organizations implemented open offices with paperless desks. As result, employees produce no papers, as there is no space to store it. Often they not even have a fixed place and sit each day on a different desk. Even if the personal contact with colleagues is still needed, working days from home or other locations is possible. So even if employees continue on the payroll (and are protected by local labor laws), many of us became already a digital

---

[98] Price, Rob (2017): "Stephen Hawking: Automatization and AI Are Going to Decimate Middle Class Jobs"

[99] Nomad List (fetched 18.8.2017)

nomad.

ACCESS GRANTED Vol.2: Tomorrow's Business Ethics

A2-24 BLOCKCHAIN TO ELIMINATE THE INTERMEDIATE

Born in 1839, Almon Brown Stowger became a school teacher after the American Civil War. As he was an introverted person, he switched the job and became an undertaker. This was an ideal work for him, as he not had much people around and further time to investigate and work on different ideas.

Normally his business was resistant to crises, but Stowger noticed that less and less people called to his office. He found the reason for this: the wife of one of his competitor's worked as a telephone-operator. She intercepted the calls for Stowger and connected them to her husband's office instead.

Due to his character, Stowger not tried to contact the telephone company and demand to fire this person, but he started to think in general about telecommunication and finally invented the "Stowger Switch", an automated telephone switching system, what could replace the job of the operator. The system eliminated the middleman (or middlewoman in this case) and the caller could select directly the receiver. A patent what he sold later in 1916 to Bell Systems.[100][101]

In the meantime intermediates stayed relevant for companies, especially in global business. This to support the organization with additional:
- technical skills
- cultural knowledge and / or
- relations.

Due to the US Foreign Corruption Practices Act from 1977, companies can held responsible for the actions of their intermediates, what can lead to high fines and even legal consequences for the involved employees. Additional to the fact that independent contractors are more difficult to control, they impose a relevant risk factor for the company. Taking on risks is essence of conducting business, so it is management decision, what levels of risk the organization is willing to accept. The benefit of an intermediate has to be compared with the potential risk factor. Different external providers can support due diligence to reduce such risk, nevertheless it is not possible to bring to 0.

Around 100 years after Stowger, a new attempt gets started to eliminate intermediate: Blockchains. The basic idea is decentralize the storage of values. Today an independent third-party is required to testify a value, for this, accounts are saved on a protected server of the bank. Blockchains aim to these intermediates. "Blocks" stand for "records" and accordingly a "Blockchain" is a "connection of records". The revolution is that these recorded values, for example a transaction, do not get recorded on particular bank server, but are distributed in the Cloud on numerous different servers. Up to now, these servers participate voluntary as they

---

[100] 99% Invisible: Episode 90: The Strowger Switch
[101] Henz, Patrick (2017): "Compliance is a Race Car."

believe in the benefit for society of this new technology. As the information is not on one single computer, but a high number of machines, it fosters data protection, as a hacker not only has to alternate information on one server, but on each of the participating computers. Together with the strong encryption of the network, this technology offers high security.

Using this technology, blockchains document the actual values. They document in real-time the financial standings of its owners. Accordingly, if their owners approve, it can be used by interested third parts for real-time monitoring. Values are more than currencies, it can also get applied for certifications and licenses. With this, it makes blockchains attractive for procurement departments. Besides prices, the potential client can have complete transparency about the providers certifications and licenses and due to this, can decide if not only the price is competitive, but also if the company has the ability to execute the project in time and quality. If blockchains get implemented for products, it would be possible for the buyer to get a better understanding not only of the ingredients, but furthermore, where they came from. Unwanted content can be identified, this can mean gluten or even new slavery and conflict minerals. Uncertainty about the claimed fair-trade get can get excluded.

Blockchain can play a key-role in the management of high-risk third-parties, such as sales agents and lobbyists. If chosen because of their technological or cultural knowledge, according certifications have to the reflect this. As long not all individuals are connected via such blockchains, the validation of personal contacts is not possible so far. But even here the technology can support, as the blockchains not only document the payments from the company to its intermediate, but also where the money came from and how the intermediate spends it later.

The question is, how far should blockchains go. As consequence of the fourth industrial wave, the implementation of AI can mean the replacement of many human job positions and drive the individuals out of regulated work. A lot of them may become micro-employees ("one-man-companies") and offer their services to different companies. Different social media platforms took on the task to bring transparency to quality, offered by craftsmen and other small companies. Users have the possibility to evaluate the commissioned services, similar to goods on ebay or Amazon. In a time where personal- and work-life merge, such evaluations could get understood not only related to quality of work, but also to the person itself. Here the blockchain technology may foster the risk, as evaluations can get more official and easier to review. Thought further, such information could influence personal credits or availability to buy or rent a home. A scenario what was already presented in the British science fiction-series Black Mirror and the episode "Nosedive".

Patrick Henz

A2-25 ETHICS, COMPLIANCE, DEMOCRACY & DATA PRIVACY ARE KEY FACTORS FOR ARTIFICIAL INTELLIGENCE

Even if the first experiments are promising, it is still not possible to let an Artificial Intelligence (AI) watch TV to get data input. Machine Learning requires an immense number of information, prepared in an understandable format. Nevertheless automation is on the rise thanks to AI and robots. As these tools require connection, information will be the key-resource, even stronger as today.

Similar to minerals, companies and countries are competing to gain access to information. This leads to new models of cooperation, as seen, for example, in the automotive sector. The competing manufacturers Audi, BMW and Daimler Benz bought as consortium the map company "Here". This to ensure a direct access to the crucial maps. Relevant for navigation systems, but furthermore also for self-driving cars. Of course, it is also strategic move around the question who will lead in future, the hardware- (car) or software-developer. The winner of this race will decide another relevant question, who will be the owner of the big amount of information, created by today's and tomorrow's cars, the hard- or software-partner. This data will push development and can cause the rise or fall of an industry.

Ethics & Compliance leads to sustainability, the same does Data Privacy. Clients (both, business and private clients) require a high level of trust to provide information. In opposite to its name "Cloud", data is not flowing through the air, but stored on servers. Especially for business clients and sensible consumer information, the server location is relevant. A country with a known restrictive and efficient data privacy law offers a competitive advantage.

But not only pure safety, also access and quality of information is imperative. For several tasks, Artificial Intelligence offers a better quality in decision making than a human employee. This requires easy access to information and adequate IT-infrastructure, but also democracy and complete & unaltered data. If the base of the decision does not show the complete picture, human and artificial decision makers will come to suboptimal results. A server location in a democratic and transparent country presents a competitive advantage.

As conclusion and besides all technological aspects, values and ethics stay relevant. With connecting different mathematical lines, it is possible to confirm all kind of relations, including a positive relation between storks and birth-rates. Important is not only to have a statistical relation, but a causal one. It is required to create "smart data" out of "big data". For this we not only need qualified employees, but as trustworthy ones. Transparency and an efficient Ethics & Compliance systems are mandatory requirements to support data processing and exude confidence to the potential clients.

ACCESS GRANTED Vol.2: Tomorrow's Business Ethics

A2-26 COMPLIANCE IS MAGIC!

Arthur C. Clarke, author of "2001: A Space Odyssey"[102] and other famous science fiction novels, once said: *"Any sufficiently advanced technology is equivalent to magic."* Besides the fast technological progress around Artificial Intelligence, the human brain is still the most advanced super computer. Magic for most of us.

New employees receive an Ethics & Compliance training shortly after their on-boarding. Often this stays their only in-person training, as the Compliance program is not changing. But such a workshop has not only the goal to inform the employees, but furthermore to motivate them and present the Compliance Officer as a trusted adviser. Only if all three aspects get reached, the individuals is able to identify dangerous situations and will contact Compliance as potential problem solver. So it is required to look for new topics to conduct additional Compliance workshops and not bore and/or lose the audience.

Such a topic could be the brain. Similar to a computer getting affected by phishing emails and viruses, also the human employee can get manipulated ("social engineering") or, based on the situation, fall to a psychological bias ("ethical blindness").

In opposite to the legal department, Compliance is about the human and due to this, wants to protect the employees, if required, even against their-selves. In other words, to avoid that good people do bad things, based on the fact that the company puts them into bad situations.

As the human psychology is highly complex, the knowledge about such biases sounds in the beginning like magic. Luckily, scientists created social experiments, which confirmed the theories. For training purposes, there are many demonstrative videos about these classic experiments, as the Stanford Prison- or the Milgram-Experiment.

---

[102] Clarke, Arthur C. (1968): "2001: A Space Odyssey"

With basing a Compliance workshop on such an experiment, we can take advantage of a psychological bias: storytelling. If we include the information inside a story, where the audience can build up empathy, they can understand and remember it much easier as if we would only present the pure information. The empathy can be related to the involved people, as they get perceived as similar to the employee or the job position; or on the other hand also with other stake holders (for example citizens in higher risk countries), as they suffer from the cost of corruption.

Important is that the employee can connect to the story/information. With this the Compliance Office can prepare them, as they learn a script "how to behave and what would be the anticipated consequences of the different choices", when they come into a similar situation.

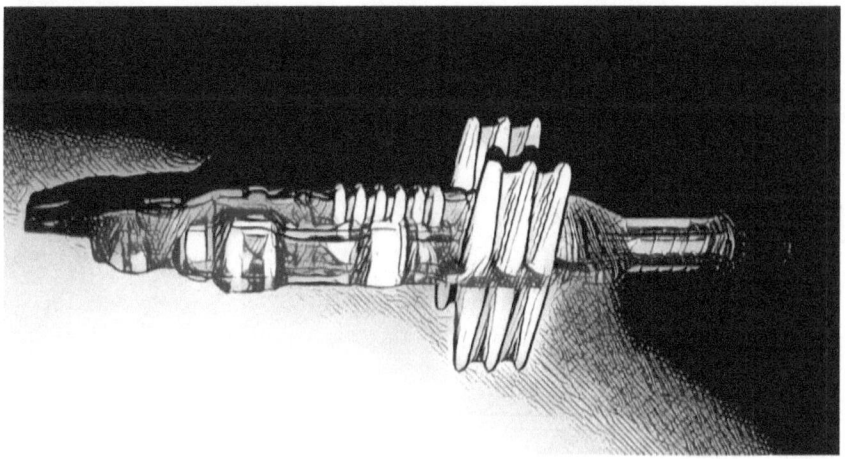

Babylon 5

The fictive space station Babylon 5 and its different civilizations explain why a global organization requires a modular approach to ensure a culture fit of the Compliance program. Besides this, B5 always had been a good example for interaction. Right from the beginning, fans started to document the different episodes in the internet. At the end of the 1990s, the web was a different place, as there was still no general access and most of the users had been students and other university personnel. In the Pre-Facebook-area, users interchanged experience in relativity closed online communities. A "Lurker" had been a passive user of such a community, who reads the different posts, but not actively posts. With this he or she had been in opposite to today's "Trolls", who use their anonymity to tell everybody in today's social platform their opinion, mostly as comment to original posts.

B5-fans collected their information on a website, the "Lurker's Guide".[103] Babylon 5-producer J. Michael Stracynski not only followed this information, but he was known to communicate with the fans in the different communities. He even included the name Lurkers later in the second season of the series, as it became the name for the people, who lived on the lower levels of stations and due to their low social levels not participated in the official life of the space station. With this the passive internet users became an active part of the TV phenomenon.

A lesson for Compliance? Yes, indeed! Training, workshops and dialogues can raise interest. This not only with extrovert, but also with introvert employees. Maybe they will not actively participate at the original event, but send later an email. The Compliance Officer can keep all discussions alive, independent, if they started in the in-person-meeting or with email. Why not create a special online-group or involve them as champions?

Today, the Lurker's Guide received its last update in 1998, but still is online, not only as the documentation of a TV-series, but also as a trip into the past of the World Wide Web.

---

[103] "The Lurker's Guide" (fetched 30.09.2017)

ACCESS GRANTED Vol.2: Tomorrow's Business Ethics

A2-27 LEMMINGS AT THE OFFICE

The British Software publisher Psygnosis introduced its game "Lemmings" in 1991 for Amiga, Atari ST and PC. The player had the task to guide the cute little green figures from their starting to the end point. As the Lemmings had no self-initiative, they limited their actions on walking and climbing. To avoid that they fall into holes or other abysses, the player had to block the way, build bridges, include ladders and more. That way a level got cleared and similar started in a more complicated environment. The game sold 15 million copies so that different sequels had been published over the next years.

As Compliance Officer, an office full of Lemmings would present a red flag. As they follow everything their management tells them, they not dare to challenge the given tasks, even if they would violate laws and guidelines.

That self-confidence, but also the opposite helplessness, are learned attributes confirmed an experiment by Martin Seligman and Steve Maier. They took dogs and separated them into three groups. The second and third groups got treated with electrical shocks. The dogs of group 2 had the possibility to stop the pain by pressing a button. The group 3 dogs had no possibility to stop this by their own behavior. For this they perceived the electrical shocks as randomly and inescapable.[104]

In a second step both scientists changed the setup of the experiment. Now all dogs of the three groups had the possibility to escape the shocks by jumping over a low partition. As it was an easy task, the dogs from the first two groups had in general no problem with it. Only the participants from the last group showed a different behavior. As they perceived the pain as something inescapable, they not even tried to escape, but stayed in their place and gave their selves in to the pain.

---

[104] Seligman, Martin / Maier, Steve (1967): "Failure to escape traumatic shock"

Self-confidence or perceived helplessness are a result of classical conditioning. Not all groups or societies have the same importance for "standing up". Similar to the presented dog experiment, also humans learn helplessness. According action and re-action, impunity is a treat to the implementation of a "stand up"-culture, independent if in society or a company. The Mexican UDLAP university published "The Global Impunity Index 2015".[105] This index gives an important overview of responses to corruption in 59 countries. Being transparent is the first step for a region, but corruption should not only be detected, but also adequately addressed. To ensure a proper corporate culture, it is imperative that potential violations receive an appropriate response, related to the wrongdoing and not to the employee's rank within the organization. No one should be above the internal guidelines. If employees do not believe this, they will not perceive compliance as a partner.

To give the Lemmings a complete make-over and turn them into confident employees requires a high and honest effort to implement a change culture. Top Management is responsible to ensure that nobody is above the organization's guidelines, the Ethics & Compliance department is the facilitator of this vision. Such a 180 degree change cannot be reached over night. It needs a longer period until all employees belief the situation that there are no more electric shocks. But the effort is worth it, as only an open corporate culture ensures compliance with values and guidelines, including usage of the whistleblower hotline, if required. For the last, employees need to trust that the company does not only not tolerates retaliation, but furthermore that an investigation wants to understand the situation and solve the potential problems:

Anticipated benefits of using the whistleblower-hotline > Anticipated costs of using the whistleblower-hotline

---

[105] Universidad de las Américas Puebla (2016): "Global Impunity Index Mexico 2016"

Patrick Henz

A2-28 KAFKA AND COMPLIANCE

Especially in the phase of a first implementation, a Compliance department may be referred to as the "dark side". At first, this in relation to the Star Wars-movies, and the picture of Darth Vader comes in mind, who tries to convince his son Luke Skywalker to join the Empire, so that both of them could rule the galaxy together.

But if you continue thinking about it, it reminds more to the dark grey world of the Czech author Franz Kafka. If a company is implementing the Compliance system as result of an actual corruption case and under time pressure, the focus will be on "detection" and "response" rather than on "prevention". For a limited time, a rules based corporate culture is required. The relation between rules & values is outside its natural equilibrium. It has a kind of irony that a company or other organization needs to ensure transparency with implementing bureaucracy.

Aachen, Germany

If the rules are established, the emphasis has to switch as soon as possible on values and attitudes, as a pure "check-the-box"-Compliance system is not sustainable and will sooner or later cause new violations, as employees perceive their-selves inside faceless processes, where at the end unknown headquarter managers decide about their requests and behavior.

As guidelines cannot define all aspects of business life, violations to external laws will happen sooner than later. Due to this, modern Compliance systems are based on controls and values, where both are inside the equilibrium. Depending on the organization this can be in the middle or a little bit more on values or a little bit more on controls.

ACCESS GRANTED Vol.2: Tomorrow's Business Ethics

A2-29 THE PERFORMANCE ZONE

The British management theorist Alasdair A. K. White defined in 2009: *"A comfort zone is a psychological state in which things feel familiar to a person and they are at ease in control of their environment, experiencing low levels of anxiety and stress. In this zone, a steady level of performance is possible"*.[106] In this state the individual receives good and even competitive results. This on a lower risk level, as all tasks are known, the challenges are limited. Based on the individual's character, this scenario is comfortable for a longer or shorter period, as the situation may become tedious. Depending on the market, the company may want to keep the employee on this level or require to push him or her outside into the performance level. Here the employee has to adapt to new scenarios and challenges. Thanks to this, the individual has the ability to grow on the job. For a limited time, the performance maybe unstable, but when fully adapted, the individual performances on a higher level. Of course, this is including a risk that the employee is not able to adapt and that the "local maximum" of the comfort zone was already the "absolute maximum" the person was capable of.

What is true for humans, applies also for software and machine learning. Even high performance computers require time to analyze big data, to convert it into smart one. The question is how much time the software should need to optimize the results. This based on the idea that after a certain time the optimizing of results with additional information not justifies the investment of further time and energy. The software stops the process, if the result complies with defined quality levels. Similar to a human employee, the app is in a "local maximum", its artificial comfort zone.

An example are GPS systems. The software calculates in seconds an ideal route, while comparing it with different other options. As a timely calculation in most of the times is more important than a route, which is

---

[106] White, Alasdair Anthony Kenneth (2009): "From Comfort Zone to Performance Management"

maybe is one or two minutes faster, the software limits the calculation for the route. So if the driver knows the way, or at least parts of it, he or she may decide to use an alternate direction. If done so, the GPS system recalculates the route and often it can be detected that thanks to this manual adaption the total travel time gets reduced for several minutes. No big differences in comparison to the earlier result, but nevertheless human experience improved machine results.

A good example how today and in future humans and AI can work together. The software will be the first line of response for a problem and, if required, the human colleague uses this as base and optimizes it.

Of course, alternate options can be the usage of an AI-only solutions. First the software creates an acceptable result to start operating. As the app operates with multi-tasking, it can in parallel continuing to calculate the best result. As scenarios are changing, it can in real-time adapt to this and calculate the new "local maximum". At the next possible situation, for example an open maintenance window, the new improved results can be included into the process.

A2-30 A YELLO FRIEND

As part of a 80's nostalgia, today Pac-Man is often remembered as Atari's most famous video-game. Less known is that in reality, he was born already in the decade before, exactly in '77; furthermore not in the US, but in Japan. Game designer Toru Iwatani invented the character, influenced by local manga and still named "Pakkuman". The name referred to the sound of opening and closing a mouth while eating.[107]

Iwatani-san created the game in his time as Namco employee, and originally for a female audience, which should had been attracted by the cute sounds and graphics. Already one year later the game became a huge success in the country and the US arcade game manufacturer Midway bought the rights to bring the yellow character into US arcades. Here the now-named "Pac-Man" took off. Only in '82 Atari published, thanks to licensing the rights from Namco, Pac-Man for the home video game console, the Atari 2600. Also thanks to the fact that they bundled the hardware with the game, Pac-Man became the best-selling home video game ever. This with around seven million sold copies. Even without Atari, the game continued its success story, as the Guinness Book of Records certified that Pac Man had been the most coin-operated arcade machines ever.

After several official successors like Ms. Pac-Man and Pac-Man Jr., it became quite around the franchise. Thanks to the introduction of the 8- and later 16-bit home computers, he received a lot of non-official brothers, as Deluxe Pac-Man or 3D Pacman for the Amiga-system. Independent game designers used the basic idea and enhanced it with modern graphics & sounds, even included pseudo and real 3D graphics. This mostly as public domain or shareware.

---

[107] Firth, Niall (2010): "Japanese inventor of Pac-Man reveals his original sketches of the iconic video game"

As the games worked thanks to its simple and addictive concept, they went on and conquered first cellular phones and then also the more sophisticated smart phones and tablets. This again directly by Namco, who released official versions for the different systems. As these devices had comparable technical abilities than the original arcade hardware, it was possible to present the game very similar to the 70's original.

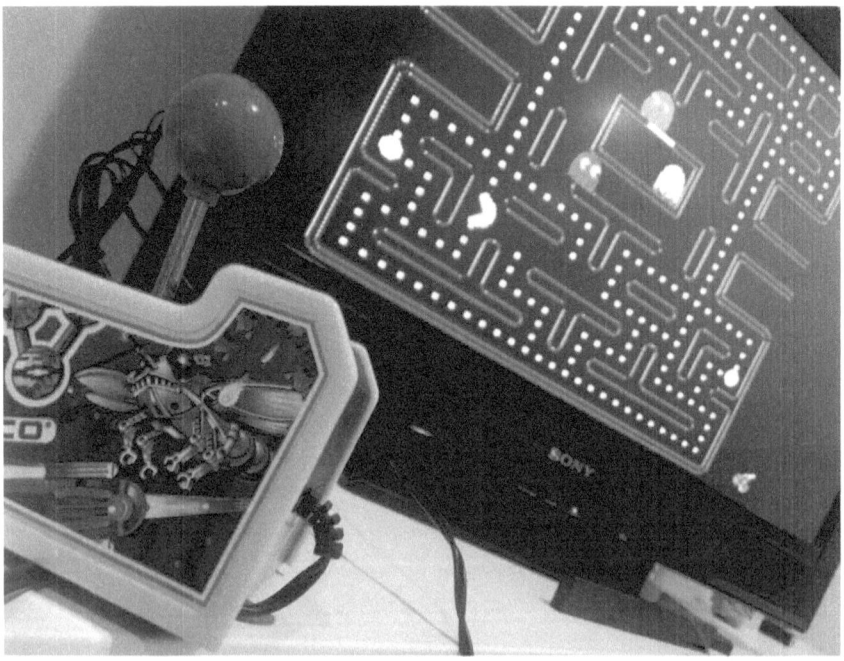

Namco used the popularity and created a retro console, which the player could directly connect to the TV and play the original Pac Man. Parallel he starred the short movie "Pixels" and in the next step went to the big silver screen to be part of the Hollywood adaption of Pixels. The last not alone, but with meeting his father Iwatani-san. At least in the story of the movie, as the game designer was interpreted by an actor.

With his latest career move, Pace Man became teacher for Artificial Intelligence. While watching the gameplay, an intelligent software learnt the rules and strategies of the game, and later could execute this better than any human player. This does not have to stay the last task for our yellow friend. Augmented Reality opens ups new possibilities, while human creativity still has not discovered all of them. What about including a virtual Pac Man into a traditional harvest corn maze or any other garden labyrinth? Such a natural fit could bring the given environment to a next level.

A2-31 VIRTUAL HERITAGE

The concept of the mid-engine opened up the possibility to create much lower cars. At the end of the 1960s, Italian designers started to play with these new possibilities and invented the wedge design. Ultra-low show cars, with a higher back than the front. The position of the engine made it possible to make the vehicles more aerodynamic than the typical front-engine cars. Creations like the Alfa Romeo Carabo, Lancia Stratos Zero and the Ferrari 512 Modulo had in common that their maximum heights had been less than one meter and furthermore they looked as coming straight out of a science fiction movie.

Even if their designs caught a lot of attention at the global expositions and by the automotive press, most of the manufacturers had not the courage to produce such a wedge car. The young Lamborghini corporation had been the exception, as they brought in 1974 the Countach to the market. The car stayed 26 years in production and for many is the brand's most remarkable product. Another wedge went in '78 into production: the BMW M1.

Even before that, the small Japanese racing company DOME CO. Ltd. started in '75 their project, the Zero. In opposite to the earlier wedge show cars, the Zero should not only be a futuristic sports car, but base for race car, ready to participate at the 24 Hours of Le Mans. Like many other manufacturers, Dome chose the Geneva Auto Show as the ideal location to present the spectacular new vehicle. In 1978 the Zero had here its first contact with the public. Nevertheless the start was not that easy, as the car could not comply with the strict Japanese homologation rules. The company manufactured one year later a more robust car, the Zero P2. Finally the car received its homologation and could get used as base for a Le Mans-version. These competed at the '79 and '80 Le Mans races, but not reached countable results, so that Dome dropped the Zero project.

1978: Dome Zero, with friendly permission from Dome Co. Ltd.

As only two drivable prototypes had been produced, most probably this remarkable wedge design car would had been forgotten, especially as Japan was an unlikely place to create such a machine. But the country had another advantage, a booming video-game industry. In 2002 Sega included the Dome Zero as special price into their Xbox title "Sega GT 2002." In the later multiplayer version, the car was selectable right from the beginning. It was not only Sega, Polyphony Digital included in 2010 the Dome Zero into their title "Gran Turismo 5". Similar to Sega, first only as price for the successful completion of special challenge and later accessible since the beginning in "Gran Turismo 6". Even if the Dome Zero is not the most competitive car in the portfolio with a total of 1200, but nevertheless fans of retro futuristic designs or especially wedge cars can select it and successfully use it for particular races and championships. Thanks to today's technical possibilities, it is not only possible to recreate famous historic buildings and cities, but prevent less known objects and circumstances from getting forgotten, or even bring them back from such a status and present them to younger generations.

Such software is not limited to reality. Manufacturers as Daimler Benz, Chrysler and Peugeot used the possibility to elaborate virtual show cars for the world of "Gran Turismo 6". This still with the idea that these vehicles could exist. Such potential connections to reality is not required, as computers can also simulate complete fictional vehicles as space ships.

A2-32 AUGMENTED VISION

Augmented Reality pushes computer reality into the user's environment, displaying it on a mobile screen or even virtual glasses. The technology can go a step further. Artificial Intelligence is about collecting information and use this as base for predictions. This related, several companies developed AI applications for the corporate hiring process. Based on psychological tests, but also gestures, the software elaborates a prediction, if the candidate is a potential fit for organization.

Even if the software is complex, it is possible to include the technology into a mobile app. The mobile application uses the smart phone only as a terminal to perceive the information. The processing of the information is inside the Cloud, where the main software not only uses the perceived information, but combines it with data from other sources. The results of the prediction gets send back to the user.

As smart devices get smaller and more difficult to identify, like fashionable smart glasses or small ear pads, this development opens up ethical pitfalls. The Swiss startup company Fennex is developing an app to use Apple's new earbuds as hearing aid.[108] A positive message for users who depend on such equipment. But such a technology could also get misused as kind of espionage-tool.

Lately, Google announced its Pixel Buds. This hardware combined with the company's smart phone should be able to translate simultaneously between 40 different languages. Especially for travelers an attractive solution. Nevertheless companies and organizations have to be careful with the usage of such a devices. As known from other voice-based devices as Alexa, Siri or Catana, all spoken information gets stored in the Cloud and analyzed by AI. With this, the provider of technology receives and stores confidential business information. This data gets used to let the AI, in this case the

---

[108] Metz, Rachel (2017): "How Your Apple Wireless Earbuds Could Double as Hearing Aids"

translator, learn. Even if the business information itself get not analyzed, the pure existence opens up the risk of leaking.

Even if electronic translators became better, they are still not perfect and their translation may include biases, for example, unintentionally disqualification of minorities. A business relation is based on trust and respect and a false word or sentence may destroy the positive work atmosphere. Learning a language and apply it later means showing respect to the local clients, and if possible should be preferred instead going the easy way and use the smart app.

Applications learn to analyze a person based on its gestures and tone of the voice. Of course, similar judgement always gets also done directly by human, but the sensitive mobile sensors combined with Artificial Intelligence may capture signals, which are undetectable by the individual and furthermore not possible to stop. If in negotiations one side might use this augmented vision, this could be an inadequate advantage.

The usage of smart lie detectors had been forecasted already at the end of last millennium by the science fiction series "Babylon 5"[109]. Not as artificial devices, but human telepaths. For important deals and closing of negotiations, business partners had the possibility to involve a commercial telepath, who ensures that all of the participants stayed with truth. In this case, the additional control was transparent and applied for all parties.

Non-necessary to mention that microphones or body-cams could not only monitor external stakeholders, but corporate headquarters could use them to control its own employees, regarding efficiency or even ensure that they would not get involved into potential bribery. This as potential buzzwords could activate an internal alarm process and inform headquarters. The technology could detect defined words, but also monitor continuously the number of words in a minute or even the meaning of sentences. Thanks to this, it could conclude what is the employee's state of mood and use this information to elaborate a sentiment analysis.

---

[109] Straczynski, J. Michael (1994): "Babylon 5"

The actual discussions around disruption often target the intermediate and try to eliminate this person, company or technology. For this, it is not surprising that computer/ and neuro-scientists already started to search for a possibility to connect the human brain directly to a computer or Cloud. With such solutions, the human individual could control smart devices with the power of thoughts, no speak or movement necessary. Of course, this opens up new ethical questions, as practically all our thoughts would be connected to the Cloud or App. Welcome to 1984! Not only the year of George Orwell's classic, but also the one where William Gibson published his novel "Neuromancer".[110] It started the "cyberpunk"-genre and practically described the possibility that humans could directly connect their-selves to a computer network, similar as Elon Tusk's Neuralink.[111]

---

[110] Gibson, William (1984): "Neuromancer"

[111] Houser, Kristin (2017): "Here's Everything You Need to Know about Elon Musk's Human/AI Brain Merge"

ACCESS GRANTED Vol.2: Tomorrow's Business Ethics

A2-33 INTERNET OF THINGS – THE GONK RISK

The Internet of Things is the actual trend to connect all smart devices to the internet, or at least a Cloud. This includes computers, laptops, phones, TVs, but also less smart devices, such as wearables, washing machines or printers. A world, where machines with different levels of intelligence co-existed already had been presented by the original 1977 Star Wars[112] movie. Of course, C-3P0 and R2-D2 had been part of the lead characters, but George Lucas created a big diversity of droids, and not all of them spoke fluently over 6 million languages as the golden robot.

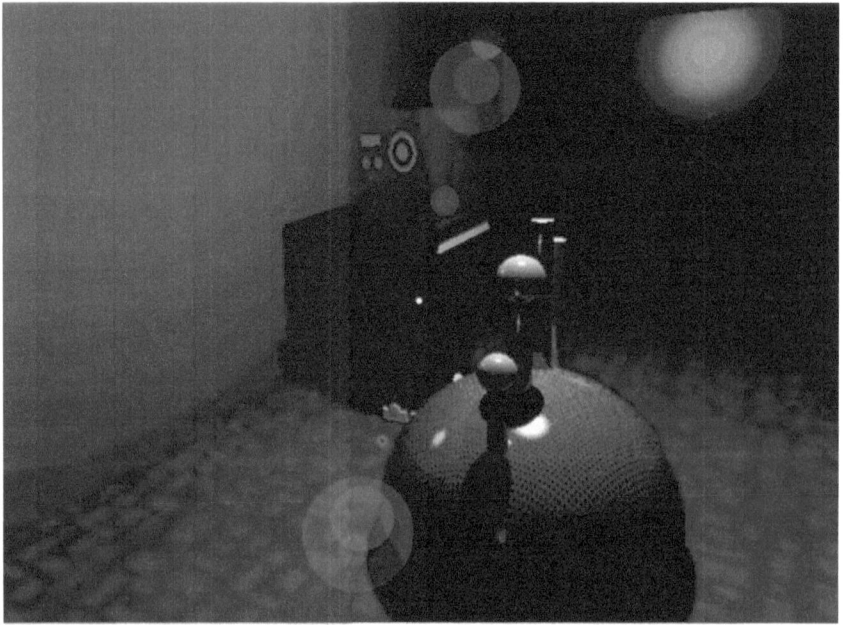

Two Droids (1997), by Patrick Henz. Left: GNK Power Droid ("Gonk"), right: LIN Droid.

Especially the power droids became a fan favorite. They are not a classic droid, more a mobile power generator. Due to this, its Artificial Intelligence was limited, what included its communication skills. The machine was only

---

[112] Lucas, George (1977): "Star Wars"

capable to produce "gonk"-like sounds, what became also the droid's nickname.

In today's networks printers are such a gonk-like device. They are connected to the Cloud for our convenience. Automatically they send a message to the manufacturer to ensure that the client receives on time the new ink. For this task the machine does not need a sophisticated AI. This make these devices vulnerable for hacker-attacks. Relevant, as users may send confidential documents wire-less to the device to print them out.

Furthermore hackers may emulate the behavior of a gonk-device, as a printer, washing machine, refrigerator or toy to get access to the network. If this is established, the faked device may get used to enter a virus into the network. Damage could be a full shut-down of the system or that the refrigerator orders food delivered to a different address. Not only a challenge for the anti-virus software, but also the user, as not all devices should get automatically added to the company- or home-network. As today's hackers not only know IT infrastructure, but furthermore also human behavior and psychological biases. They often identified the human employee as the weak brick inside the firewall. A raising level of Industry 4.0 requires that employers ensure that their employees get smarter to not become a gonk.

A2-34 … AND ENDS.

In 2017, Elon Musk (Tesla), Mustafa Suleyman (Alphabet) and a long list of other AI and robotics specialists signed an open letter to the United Nations Convention on Certain Conventional Weapons: *"Lethal autonomous weapons threaten to become the third revolution in warfare. Once developed, they will permit armed conflict to be fought at a scale greater than ever, and at timescales faster than humans can comprehend. These can be weapons of terror, weapons that despots and terrorists use against innocent populations, and weapons hacked to behave in undesirable ways. We do not have long to act. Once this Pandora's box is opened, it will be hard to close."*[113]

Again, we can link this vision to a story by Philip K. Dick: "Second Variety"[114] from 1953. A long lasting war has swiped out most parts of mankind and at the end the last soldiers are fighting against self-replicating robots. In 1995 the story was used for the movie "Screamers".

If we are thinking of an AI defense system, the programmers surely want to protect it against enemy hackers and make it as difficult as possible to destroy or hijack the system. This can be achieved by using modern software architecture, not have it run on one particular server, but distribute it via a cloud over different servers. It can go a step further, parts of the defense system can work like a virus program: move from computer to computer and even multiply if different parts require additional computing power. Needless to say that once activated, it would be very difficult to deactivate such a defense program and may stay active even after the conflict. A final war between mankind and machines would be the result. A warning sign are land mines, which mean a deadly menace even decades after the original war.

---

[113] 2017: "An Open Letter to the United Nations Convention on Certain Conventional Weapons"

[114] Dick, Philip. K (1953): "Second Variety"

Patrick Henz

BIBLIOGRAPHY

- 2017: "An Open Letter to the United Nations Convention on Certain Conventional Weapons": https://www.cse.unsw.edu.au/~tw/ciair//open.pdf
- 99% Invisible: Episode 90: The Strowger Switch: http://99percentinvisible.org/episode/strowger-switch-purple-reign-redux/
- Aharoni, Eyal / Vincent, Gina M. / Harenski, Carla L. / Calhoun, Vince D. / Sinnott-Armstrong, Walter / Gazzaniga, Michael, S. / Kiehl, Kent A. (2012): "Neuroprediction of future rearrest": http://www.pnas.org/content/110/15/6223.full
- Brain Box (2015): "What does fMRI measure?": http://the-brain-box.blogspot.com/2015/05/what-does-fmri-measure.html
- Chiang, Ted (1998): "The Story of Life"
- Clarke, Arthur C. (1968): "2001: A Space Odyssey"
- Clifton, Brian / Lavigne, Sam / Tseng, Francis (2017): "Predicting Financial Crime: Augmenting the Predictive Policing Arsenal": https://whitecollarcrime.zone/static/whitepaper.pdf
- Cooper, Daniel (2015): "Google's newest AI can beat your Atari highs-scores": https://www.engadget.com/2015/02/26/deepmind-atari-games-tests/
- Crassey, David (1973): "Other People's Money: A Study in the Social Psychology of Embezzlement"
- deGrasse Tyson, Neil (2017): "Astrophysics for People in a Hurry"
- Deming, William Edwards (1986): "Out the Crisis"
- Deming, William Edwards (2000): "The New Economics for Industry, Governance, Education"
- Dent, Steve (2017): "Humans can help AI learn games more quickly": https://www.engadget.com/2017/06/07/humans-can-help-ai-learn-games-more-quickly/
- Dick, Philip. K (1953): "Second Variety"
- Dick, Philip K. (1956): "The Minor:ity Report"
- Dick, Philip K. (1966): "Total Recall"
- Dick, Philip K. (1968): "Do Androids Dream of Electric Sheep?"
- Diffen (fetched 16.11.2017): "Accountability vs. Responsibility": https://www.diffen.com/difference/Accountability_vs_Responsibility
- Ethereum (2017): "Blockchain App Platform": https://www.ethereum.org/
- EUGDPR (2017): "GDPR Portal": http://www.eugdpr.org/
- Firth, Niall (2010): "Japanese inventor of Pac-Man reveals his original sketches of

- the iconic video game": http://www.dailymail.co.uk/sciencetech/article-1289239/Japanese-inventor-Pac-Man-reveals-original-sketches-iconic-video-game.html
- Fogel, Stefanie (2017): "EVE Online is crowdsourcing the search for real exoplanets": https://www.engadget.com/2017/02/22/eve-online-project-discovery-exoplanets/
- Galouye, Daniel F. (1964): "Simulacron-3"
- Gibson, William (1984): "Neuromancer"
- Google Cardboard (fetched 28.08.2017): https://vr.google.com/cardboard/
- Hartsthorne, Joshua (2009): "Does Language Shape What We Think?": https://www.scientificamerican.com/article/does-language-shape-what/
- Henz, Patrick (2016): Business Philosophy according to Enzo Ferrari"
- Henz, Patrick (2017): "Access Granted – Tomorrow's Business Ethics"
- Henz, Patrick (2017): "Compliance is a Race Car."
- Henz, Patrick (2017): "Wirtschaftspsychologie und Compliance"
- Hoffman, Billy (2017): "Hacking as Cognitive Skills": https://www.youtube.com/watch?v=UWX7sS7a0mU
- Hogan-Brun, Gabrielle (2017): "People who speak multiple languages make the best employees for one big reason": https://qz.com/927660/people-who-speak-multiple-languages-make-the-best-employees-for-one-big-reason/
- Houser, Kristin (2017): "Here's Everything You Need to Know about Elon Musk's Human/AI Brain Merge": https://futurism.com/heres-everything-you-need-to-know-about-elon-musks-humanai-brain-merge/
- Howell, Elizabeth (2016): "Parallel Universes: Theories & Evidence": https://www.space.com/32728-parallel-universes.html
- Jones, Rhett (2017): „NFL Players Strike a Deal to Sell Their Biometric Data":http://gizmodo.com/nfl-players-strike-a-deal-to-sell-their-biometric-data-1794616994?utm_campaign=socialflow_gizmodo_twitter&utm_source=gizmodo_twitter&utm_medium=socialflow

- Kasparov, Garry (2010): "The Chess Master and the Computer": http://www.nybooks.com/articles/2010/02/11/the-chess-master-and-the-computer/
- Keohane, Joe (2017): "What new-writing bots mean for the future of journalism": https://www.wired.com/2017/02/robots-wrote-this-story/
- Knight, Will (2017): "An Algorithm Summarizes Lengthy Text Surprisingly Well": https://www.technologyreview.com/s/607828/an-algorithm-summarizes-lengthy-text-surprisingly-well/
- Koch, Hannes (2017): "Crowdworker – die Wanderarbeiter der digitalen Generation": https://www.morgenpost.de/berlin-aktuell/startups/article210331363/Crowdworker-die-Wanderarbeiter-der-digitalen-Generation.html
- Lawgeex.com (fetched 16.05.2017): "features": https://www.lawgeex.com/features/

- Lazzaro, Sage (2017): "Look, no hands! $399 camera necklace lets you livestream videos directly to Facebook, Instagram, and YouTube without lifting a finger": http://www.dailymail.co.uk/sciencetech/article-4797486/Camera-necklace-stream-videos-directly-social-media.html
- Lincoln, Abraham (1862): "Annual Message to the Congress": http://www.abrahamlincolnonline.org/lincoln/speeches/congress.htm
- Lovelock, James (1972): "Gaia as seen through the atmosphere"
- Lucas, George (1977): "Star Wars"
- Machiavelli, Niccolò (1513): "Il Principe"
- Martin, Jennifer L. (fetched 29.4.2017): "Travel & Jet Lag": http://www.sleephealthylivewell.com/Travel___Jet_Lag.html
- Maslow, Abraham (1943): "A Theory of Human Motivation"
- Mellino, Cole (2016): "The World's Largest Earth Science Experiment: Biosphere 2": http://www.ecowatch.com/the-worlds-largest-earth-science-experiment-biosphere-2-1882107636.html
- Metz, Rachel (2017): "How Your Apple Wireless Earbuds Could Double as Hearing Aids": https://www.technologyreview.com/s/608597/how-your-apple-wireless-earbuds-could-double-hearing-aids/?utm_campaign=Owned+Social&utm_source=Twitter&utm_medium=Owned+Social
- Metz, Rachel (2017): "Now There's a Nausea Dial for Virtual Reality": https://www.technologyreview.com/s/608709/now-theres-a-nausea-dial-for-virtual-reality/
- Microsoft (fetched 08.11.2017): Microsoft Workplace Analytics: https://products.office.com/en-us/business/workplace-analytics
- Mohomed, Carimo (2011): "The abolition of the Past: History in George Orwell's 1984": http://www.ipedr.com/vol17/13-CHHSS%202011-H00048.pdf
- National Institute of Standards and Technology (2014): "Framework for Improving Critical Infrastructure Cybersecurity": https://www.nist.gov/sites/default/files/documents/cyberframework/cybersecurity-framework-021214.pdf
- Nomad List (fetched 18.8.2017): https://nomadlist.com/
- Orwell, George (1949): "1984"
- Phys.org (2017): "The elements of life mapped across the Mily Way by SDSS/APOGEE": https://phys.org/news/2017-01-elements-life-milky-sdssapogee.html
- Price, Rob (2017): "Stephen Hawking: Automatization and AI Are Going to Decimate Middle Class Jobs": https://futurism.com/stephen-hawking-automation-and-ai-is-going-to-decimate-middle-class-jobs/
- Prior, Ryan (2017): Your next job interview could be with a recruiter bot.": http://money.cnn.com/2017/05/16/technology/ai-recruiter-mya-systems/index.html?sr=twcnni051617ai-recruiter-mya-systems0312PMStoryLink&linkId=37640206
- Racz, Niclas / Weippl, Edgar / Seufert, Andreas (2010): A Frame of Reference for

Research of Integrated Governance, Risk and Compliance (GRC)
- Sagan, Carl (1980): "Cosmos"
- Scott, Ridley (1979): "Alien"
- Scott, Ridley (1982): "Blade Runner"
- Seligman, Martin / Maier, Steve (1967): "Failure to escape traumatic shock"
- sky.foofighters.com (2017): "Sky is a Neighborhood": sky.foofighters.com
- The Alan Turing Internet Scrapbook (2014): "The Turing Test, 1950": http://www.turing.org.uk/scrapbook/test.html
- The Economist (2017): "The kids are alright": http://www.economist.com/node/12591038?fsrc=scn/tw/te/bl/ed/thekidsarealright
- The Rosetta Project (fetched 21.06.2017): https://rosettaproject.org/about/
- Sayej, Nadja (2017): "This Old School Wearable Puts a Thousand Languages Around Your Neck": https://motherboard.vice.com/en_us/article/this-old-school-wearable-puts-a-thousand-languages-around-your-neck
- Silverman, Rachel Emma (2000): "The Words of Tomorrow": https://www.wsj.com/millennium/articles/SB944517141695981261.htm
- Simonite, Tom (2017): "Microsoft Masters Ms. Pac-Man with a Horde of AI Agents": https://www.wired.com/story/mircosoft-ai-ms-pac-man/
- Stanford University (fetched 22.05.2017): "Stanford Persuasive Tech Lab": http://captology.stanford.edu/
- StarTalk Radio (2017): "The Science of Creativity, with David Byrne": https://soundcloud.com/startalk/the-science-of-creativity-with-david-byrne?utm_source=soundcloud&utm_campaign=wtshare&utm_medium=Twitter&utm_content=https%3A//soundcloud.com/startalk/the-science-of-creativity-with-david-byrne
- Statt, Nick (2016): "Adobe is working on an audio app that lets you add words someone never said": https://www.theverge.com/2016/11/3/13514088/adobe-photoshop-audio-project-voco
- Stoecker, Christian (2017): "Werden Sie Teil der Maschine": http://www.spiegel.de/wissenschaft/technik/digitale-ueberredungstechnik-laesst-menschen-nach-ihrer-pfeife-tanzen-a-1148463.html
- Straczynski, J. Michael (1994): "Babylon 5"
- The Lurker's Guide (fetched 30.09.2017): http://www.midwinter.com/lurk/toc.html
- Tushman, Michael L. / Kahn, Anna / Porray, Mary Elizabeth / Binns, Andy (2017): "Email and Calendar Data Are Helping Firms Understand How Employees Work": https://hbr.org/2017/08/email-and-calendar-data-are-helping-firms-understand-how-employees-work?utm_campaign=hbr&utm_source=twitter&utm_medium=social
- Tversky, Amos / Kahnemann, Daniel (1974): "Judgment under Uncertainty: Heuristics and Biases"
- Universidad de las Américas Puebla (2016): "Global Impunity Index Mexico 2016": http://www.udlap.mx/igimex/assets/files/igimex2016_ENG.pdf

- Villeneuve, Denis (2016): "Arrival"
- Villeneuve, Denis (2017): "Blade Runner 2049"
- Vincent, James (2017): "Lyrebird claims it can recreate any voice using just one minute of sample audio": https://www.theverge.com/2017/4/24/15406882/ai-voice-synthesis-copy-human-speech-lyrebird
- WashPostPR (2016): "The Washington Post experiments with automated storytelling to help power 2016 Rio Olympics coverage": https://www.washingtonpost.com/pr/wp/2016/08/05/the-washington-post-experiments-with-automated-storytelling-to-help-power-2016-rio-olympics-coverage/?utm_term=.2cb270dac701
- Weller, Chris (2017): "A neuroscientist who studies decision-making reveals the most important choice you can make.": https://www.weforum.org/agenda/2017/08/a-neuroscientist-who-studies-decision-making-reveals-the-most-important-choice-you-can-make?utm_content=bufferde9c3&utm_medium=social&utm_source=twitter.com&utm_campaign=buffer
- Wells, Herbert George (1898): "The War of the Worlds"
- White, Alasdair Anthony Kenneth (2009): "From Comfort Zone to Performance Management"
- Woyke, Elizabeth (2017): "The Enduring Legacy of Zork": https://www.technologyreview.com/s/608670/the-enduring-legacy-of-zork/
- www.fatml.org (2017): "Fairness, Accountability, and Transparency in Machine Learning"
- www.michael-schumacher.de (fetched 11.08.2017): "Giving Back": http://www.michael-schumacher.de/en/giving-back/
- Yang, Yuan (2017): "China seeks glimpse of citizens' future with crime-predicting AI": https://www.ft.com/content/5ec7093c-6e06-11e7-b9c7-15af748b60d0
- YouTube (2009): "Responsibility vs Accountability": https://www.youtube.com/watch?time_continue=163&v=NZJ3Nw60CKs
- ZDF (2017): "Gladiatoren im Kollosseum": http://vr.zdf.de/gladiatoren/

ACCESS GRANTED – Tomorrow's Business Ethics

"ACCESS GRANTED – Tomorrow's Business Ethics" is science fiction in its literally sense. The book analyzes actual and future technological developments to discuss how these will affect tomorrow's business reality and its impact on the human.

It is clear that robotization and the implementation of Artificial Intelligence will change companies and societies. This does not mean automatically a shift for the better or worse, but life will be different, and it is in our hands to use technology for the first.

Artificial Intelligence, robots, 3D printing, micro-learnings, virtual reality, self-driving cars and all other autonomous software and machines will be a part of tomorrow's business. We have to start thinking about the consequences. A chance and challenge for management, where the Ethics&Compliance-department can position itself as a key-player and include AI inside its responsibilities.

ACCESS GRANTED Vol.2: Tomorrow's Business Ethics

First edition, 154 pages. ISBN-10: 1544849826. ISBN-13: 978-1544849829.

ABOUT THE AUTHOR

Patrick Henz started his career in Corporate Information and Compliance at the end of 2007, when he was responsible for the implementation of an Anti-Corruption program in Mexico and several Central American and Caribbean countries. Together with these tasks, he gained valuable insights into global Compliance programs, with a focus on Latin America. Since 2009 in his role as Compliance Officer he is responsible for an effective Compliance program; based on identification, protection, detection, response & recovery and combined with integrity, respect, passion & sustainability. With these means, he defines Compliance as pro-active function, being perceived as guardian, expert and facilitator. The focus is on information to ensure adequate behavior, not only of the human employee, but Artificial Intelligence included.

This includes the regular planning and execution of Compliance Risk Assessments and further global reviews. According an effective sustainability strategy, where Compliance plays a key role, he actively promotes this idea at university workshops and conferences (including the ACI Compliance Boot-Camp 2013, '15 and '17 in Houston). In so doing he became two times President of Honor of Marcus Evans' Latin-American Corporate Compliance Conference 2011 and '12 in Mexico City, panelist at The Economist's Mexico Summit 2015 and co-founder of the Ethics & Compliance Forum Mexico, including editor and co-author of the Ethics & Compliance Manual, published in April 2014.

Since 2013 he lives and works in Atlanta, USA.

www.ingramcontent.com/pod-product-compliance
Lightning Source LLC
Chambersburg PA
CBHW031415210526
45464CB00005B/1901